OUTSWIMMING

THE GREY HOUND

by

Mike Wells

This book is dedicated to the sensitive souls who struggle for wellbeing in difficult times.

[Modern man and woman is] blind to the fact that, with all his rationality and efficiency, he is possessed by 'powers' that are beyond his control. His gods and demons have not disappeared at all; they have merely got new names. They keep him on the run with restlessness, vague apprehensions, psychological complications, an insatiable need for pills, alcohol, tobacco, food — and, above all, a large array of neuroses.

KARL JUNG

INTRODUCTION-BOND

If you fall during your life, it doesn't matter. You're never a failure as long as you try to get up.

– Evel Knievel

The sun is beating down. I'm at the helm of a powerboat, a great long phallus of a thing, speeding across the ocean. The craft is gracefully leaping wave to wave. Behind me in the cockpit are three beautiful women, their long hair flowing in the breeze as the boat charges forward. They adore me, and not just for my money and lifestyle, which is one even James Bond might envy.

We approach some rocks. I daringly steer the boat between them at fifty miles an hour. My friend, who also has a bevy of bikini-clad women aboard, takes his boat on a wider, safer curve outside the rocks. Both boats enter a bay and we slow to walking pace before dropping anchor, my friend mooring alongside me. As the sun goes down we sip Martini with ice and lemon. There are smiles, good conversation, flirting.

How dumb was I? I thought my life would be like the adverts I watched as a kid. You can imagine my disappointment when instead of the James Bond lifestyle of soft-focus glamour, and gentle sips of Martini on the rocks, I wind up personally on the rocks, living on a rusting little boat in London's grimy backwaters, sculling back red wine like there was no tomorrow.

I was brought up in an affluent, socially mobile family in a picturesque village in Sussex. You could say I started at the top and worked my way down. But according to Evel Knievel's measure I'm not a complete failure, because despite falling, I keep on getting back up.

Now, as the property-owning classes surf the wave, and the box-set watching masses munch posh crisps on their comfy sofas, I find myself doing neither. Nor are there any long-haul flights to exotic holiday destinations to rejuvenate my batteries ready for another round in my demanding yet well-paid job. That's because there is no well-paid job. Looks like I've failed to meet my key performance indicators – no kids, no nice home, and no wife. I'm a failure at all that sort of stuff, so I've invented my own job – writing this book.

Some people write about growing up, others about ageing. This book is about both. If I live to finish this story, and if you live to finish reading it, you might get my drift. Often depressed, dishevelled, divorced, dyslexic, a down-shifter in denial about death, that's me.

LIDO

This life is like a swimming pool. You dive into the water, but you can't see how deep it is.
DENIS RODMAN

I submerge my goggle-clad head and smile as I watch rays of light streak through the water and constantly changing shadows of wavelets copying themselves onto the pool bottom, while surface-seeking bubbles sparkle like diamonds. My mood instantly lifts.

The swimming habit started unintentionally. Living on a boat with finite water supplies, it made sense to go to the lido, if only to use the shower. And the lido at London Fields, being located centrally between my boat's different mooring spots, meant that I would never have to cycle more than half an hour to reach it. Unexpectedly, swimming quickly became the highlight of my day. Afterwards I felt calmer, more relaxed and less depressed. A lido may not benefit from the distant horizons of the sea, but importantly, like the ocean, it has no roof, allowing the sun-deprived city dweller to synthesise much-needed vitamin D.

On hot summer days this is the place to be seen. The full range of human skin colours are on display as the multicultural populace of the capital congregate poolside, the water itself just a backdrop for socialising and flirting. The water is heated to 26 °C, and in the winter it steams comfortingly when, in the absence of revellers, the only sound is churning water echoing from the walls of lockers, while bored lifeguards in their lookout towers pretend they aren't daydreaming.

There are four lanes. One for folks who just want to splash about, and three others marked 'slow', 'medium' and 'fast'. The testosterone quotient varies accordingly. Beware the fast lane, where the imperative for speed overrides any sense of courtesy and barging is common. I'm a middle-lane swimmer. But to glide forwards through water your body needs to be straight, pointing in the direction of travel. After all, an arrow doesn't fly sideways. I'm not at all arrow like. It's frustrating – a challenge I feel compelled to take up.

***

Do you know that one of the great problems of our age is that we are governed by people who care more about feelings than they do about thoughts and ideas.

MARGARET THATCHER

The fact of the matter is that getting in the water at the lido has prevented me sinking altogether. I often wonder how many of the other swimmers feel the same.

The notion of public wellbeing is why these outdoor pools were built. London was an important centre both of the need for lidos and the actuality of constructing them. Janet Smith, in her book on lidos, *Liquid Assets*, reports that between the early 1900s and 1951, around sixty were built across the capital; more, relative to population, than anywhere else in the country. Herbert Morrison, chair of the London County Council (LCC) from 1934 to 1940, epitomised this spirit when he promised to turn the metropolis into 'a city of lidos', pledging that no Londoner would have to walk more than a mile and a half to their nearest one.

The title of Janet Smith's book juxtaposes two ideologies: those of Herbert Morrison and Margaret Thatcher. The latter's policies of liquidating the liquid assets has reduced the number of lidos in London from sixty to nine, and caused their wholesale closure elsewhere across the nation. London Fields was one such casualty, but thanks to the tenacity of local campaigners this asset reopened and is back in the business of helping people like me maintain buoyancy in difficult times.

RABIES

Industry without art is brutality.

ANANDA K. COOMARASWAMY

One day I walk out of the lido changing room to find a posse of poolside workers. Bizarrely, one of them is sitting behind a desk peering into a CCTV monitor. There are wires and gadgets everywhere and a hose running into the pool. On the end of it I'm surprised to see a diver. He's checking for loose tiles, tapping all 40,000 of them with a little hammer. I can hear the dull thudding of his hammer while swimming.

I love metaphors, and here was a good one. We industrial humans are like those tiles. The System wants us to line up in neat rows and conform, but in straining to do so many of us become *loose*, and when something taps on our soul all we can do is make a dull, hollow sound.

Carl Jung talks of the modern era's obsession with averaging. Science, he notes, uses averaging to model the physical world, but in reality such averages are unlikely to exist. Rather than tiles, in *The Undiscovered Self*, Jung uses the analogy of a batch of stones. If their total weight is divided by the number of stones, an average weight for each stone will be derived, but of course it's unlikely any of the stones will actually conform to this average. Likewise, despite all attempts to reduce them to numbers humans rarely conform to an average, either physically or psychologically. While science and systems of batch processing may have brought benefits, we need to acknowledge like Jung that this often comes at a cost.

***

Right from the beginning it was obvious my relationship with the System was going to be tricky. At school I was a spork in a draw full of conventional cutlery, my spelling was unique and my maths didn't add up, but a far bigger problem was an inability to sit still. Today they'd say I had ADHD.

A normal day. My classmates look alarmed. Our teacher has just thrown a metre-long ruler at me. It scythes through the air past the studious kids in the front and middle rows. I feel the wind as it sails past my ear. He misses, and the ruler clatters harmlessly to the floor at the back of our batch's allocated processing area (aka classroom). It goes quiet. For a moment the teacher in turn looks alarmed at his own loss of control.

He makes his way over to me at the back of the classroom. Close up I can see his eyes bulging and there's froth at the corners of his mouth. The guy's displaying all the symptoms of rabies. Head thrust forward, he stands in front of me shouting, declaring me a dismal failure. His halitosis makes me want to back away, but I'm trapped.

What's wrong with you, I wonder. Why are you so angry about something that doesn't matter? I wasn't an average child. I was well below average. The pedagogue's blood pressure had shot up to a life-threatening level because I'd got nothing right in his mock exam. I hadn't even spelt my own name correctly.

I wanted to believe that I couldn't have cared less about his temper tantrum. But I now realise the cumulative impact of these sorts of incidents was a form of conditioning. ADHD, and dyslexia, and being an annoying prick made me difficult to teach.

It wasn't deliberate. I didn't enjoy being annoying. But with no power and no voice and being so frequently humiliated I lost respect for most teachers and most adults. In eleven years at school I only learned one thing, which was drilled into me many times a day: *don't trust authority.*

Jung wrote *The Undiscovered Self* in the 1950s. Since then the batch processing problem has become more potent. Our minds are fed with marketing and entertainment designed to convince us of our individuality, while at the same time educators, employers and bureaucrats treat us like the nuts and bolts in the machinery of their averaged world. The messages are contradictory – to be a sausage in the factory, but at the same time to be an individual.

Procrustes is a character from Greek mythology. A blacksmith and a bandit, he would trick travellers into spending the night at his gaff. While they were asleep he'd tie his guests to his iron bed. Too tall for the bed and he'd cut their legs to fit. Too short and he'd stretch them. No one fitted his bed; they all perished.

Living with the cultural contradictions of our age, I feel like I'm strapped to a Procrustean bed with my psyche being stretched to its limit, and I know I'm not alone. I can see some folks whose strategy for survival is to amputate their souls as a means of coping. And many others, including myself, are using alcohol and drugs as a means of doing something similar. It's like the emperor's new clothes. Except we are all the emperor, and no one's laughing.

Aged thirteen I certainly wasn't laughing, I knew I wasn't OK. Emotionally disturbed, confused and angry, grappling with feelings and a world which made no sense, with no role models to help, so I did what many crazy mixed-up kids do, I started drinking. I was out of control and an absolute pain in the arse. Decades later, I realise denial, repression and alcohol have achieved nothing.

ENTREPRENEUR

It is best to act with confidence, no matter how little right you have to it.

LILLIAN HELLMAN

Immersion in water has a similar quality to the weightlessness of outer space. That, and its otherworldliness, is why astronauts train under water. The feeling of getting into a warm bath, the water wrapping herself round you in an amniotic embrace, says more than words ever can. Yet outside the confines of a bath, water also has the ability to open the floodgates of terror. The nightmare of drowning, the discomfort of cold, the horror of sea and loch monsters, and an infinite number of other real and imagined dangers.

The next step up from the lido is the sea. So, pushing my boundaries, swimming alone off the beach at Blackpool Sands – which is neither sandy nor in Blackpool, it's on the South Devon coast – I look up to get my bearings and notice a grey-headed swimmer close by. I swim on. Then it occurs to me, that was an odd-looking head, all grey and dome shaped. I stop and look again. No one. I feel a surge of panic as I imagine a dome-headed creature sinking its teeth into the soft skin of my belly. 'Stay calm,' I say to myself and continue – a bit faster and a lot more nervous. It was probably a seal.

I would never have been able to swim in the sea like this a year ago. Swimming at the lido is gradually rebuilding my confidence, in and out of the water.

***

Thousands Have Lived Without Love, Not One Without Water.

W.H. AUDEN

A completely dry human would shrivel to a mere 30 per cent of their wet weight. Centres of population have traditionally been established at fords, bridges, rivers and natural harbours. Water is in our cells, our souls and our landscapes. Even in the desert, water makes itself significant by its scarcity.

Proximity to water is also an arena in the arms race of status symbols: a swimming pool in a west London basement, a second home on the coast, the competition between oligarchs to have the stupidest super-yacht. For those of us not on the list of high net worth individuals, the coast has always pulled in holidaying workers, while property magnates turn waterside developments into gold as over-financed punters queue up to buy apartments with Juliet balconies overlooking the canals and rivers on which my boat floats.

Rainbows, mermaids, nymphs; baptisms and the pagan ritual of well dressing: water is embedded in our culture. And it looks like water can even soften a heart like mine, which I thought had turned to stone.

***

Never put off till tomorrow what may be done the day after tomorrow just as well.

MARK TWAIN

My life is a back catalogue of near misses – a near drowning while windsurfing, motorcycle crashes and other stupidities – but despite these near-death experiences I cling to the denial of death like I clung to the wall of an Alpine ravine I accidentally fell into. That is until a couple of weeks ago, when nature gave me a wake-up call.

My boat was moored on the River Lea at Walthamstow Marshes, where the only clue that you are in the midst of a city of epic proportions are the trains that frequently rattle their way across this wide open space. A blue plaque attached to an arch on the bridge which carries those trains across the river announces that 'near this spot in 1909 Alliott Verdon Roe built and flew the first powered aircraft in Britain'.

Like metaphors, another of my quirks is to imagine meeting people from the past. And so it was as I cycled home across this open landscape, passing under the blue plaque bridge, that in my mind's eye I could see Alliott Roe and myself strolling across the marshes. He in blue overalls and white scarf, his hair neatly cut, looking every bit the showman.

'Mike,' he says, pointing skywards towards the airliners turning on their long final approach into Heathrow, 'what the hell are those?'

'Well Alliot,' I say, waving in the direction of his former workshop under the arches, 'since you built your airplane the technology has progressed.' I point up. 'Those aircraft carry millions of people a year and fly at five hundred miles an hour all over the world. And the fastest planes fly at twice the speed of sound.'

He's visibly shocked. He pushes his flat cap back over his well-coiffured head and strokes his clean-shaven chin.

'But they don't have propellers,' he says.

I continue, 'They're used for carrying people, cargo and bombs.'

At the word ‘bombs’ he turns and looks me in the eye.

‘Yes,’ I say. ‘The Germans used airplanes to drop thousands of tons of bombs on London between 1940 and 1944.’ Alliot’s jaw drops. ‘But we dropped even more on them,’ I say.

‘Why?’ he asks.

I’m unsure how to respond. I know more about his future than he does. He doesn’t know the First World War is going to happen, let alone the Second. His thinking is embedded in a different era, so it would be difficult to explain that his support for fascism is doomed and that he’ll endure the loss of two sons fighting it. Both of them will follow in their dad’s footsteps and become pilots in the RAF, both to be killed in action, their bodies never recovered.

This knowledge makes me feel awkward; it’s time to wrap up this conversation. ‘Dude, I’ll see you on the other side,’ I say, and he dissolves back into the crowded hinterland of the dead.

Arriving home, I chain my bicycle to the rail around the back deck. As I do it starts buzzing and crackling with electrical energy. I’m confused. The boat isn’t connected to the mains. I drop the lock for fear of electrocution and there’s a deafening explosion. My heart hits the inside of my ribcage. I jump back and glance down at myself, half expecting to see bits missing. But I’m intact and there’s no blood. I look around and into the distance. No sign of anything out of the ordinary.

I realise the roulette wheel of fortune has favoured me. Out of that same sky through which Alliot Roe flew a century ago has come a bolt of lightning which must have struck the boat’s chimney, the highest point within a few hundred metres. I look up at the clouds: cumulo-nimbus (Thunder clouds). In my mind’s eye

I see a smoking pair of canvas sneakers – my sneakers, all that's left of me. Unlike Alliot Roe I don't get a blue plaque.

***

People that keep stiff upper lips find that it's hard to smile.

JUDITH GUEST

It was my well-read friend Richy who suggested reading Roger Deakin's *Waterlog*, an account of it's author's wild swimming in various locations around the country. The book starts with its writer swimming the moat around his house, suggesting that his home was actually a castle. The moat, and his style of writing, makes me think he was posh, but it wasn't the poshness that bothered me, it was a quality commonly associated with the British upper classes – the stiff upper lip, and those lips' difficulty in expressing emotion. I wanted to know how swimming made its author feel, but he wasn't giving much away.

A far more entertaining read is 'The Swimmer', a short story by John Cheever, which inspired Deakin to write *Waterlog*. 'Cheever's', protagonist swims his way across a series of pools belonging to the residents of his bourgeois suburb. During his adventure he wonders if some misfortune has befallen one of his neighbours. Their house is boarded up, a For Sale sign nailed to a tree in the front garden, its pool empty and full of dead leaves.

Was his memory failing or had he so disciplined it in the repression of unpleasant facts that he had damaged his sense of truth?

When I read this sentence, embedded within a narrative of mental ill-health, I was brought up short. That's what I've been doing, attempting to repress the unpleasant facts of life, to blot them out with alcohol and drugs. And in so doing I've damaged my sense of truth. There have been times when my very sense of self has become blurred, as though I was seeing the world and myself through a frosted window.

The repression approach, like so many bottles I've drained, is empty and without substance. It's become clear that booze and drugs aren't the solution – they are the problem. I can feel repressed emotions pushing at the doors of my resilience.

'The Swimmer' and *Waterlog* planted the seed of an idea to write a book about swimming and more importantly my feelings about swimming. The fertiliser for the growth of this seed is the deadness of their authors. Procrastination til death would be a waste.

***

Big Ben, News at Ten, important men, cufflinks and pinstripe, it's all hype, but nothing beguiles coz there ain't no smiles.
They're in it for the high pay, getting it made in Taipei, not caring who they slay.
Status anxiety dystopia it must be some kinda myopia.
Volcanoes, violence, and vendettas.
Plane crash and murder for cash, tidal waves, tsunamis and terror on the airwaves.
We're all in the news man's hands. You can't be deaf to his stories of death.
Walking wounded depressed, suppressed by the advertiser's collusion with delusion.
Head in hand, or in the sand, it's enough to make you go mad.

Booze isn't the only problem. My home town of London, as well as being a centre of politics, finance and enterprise, should also be seen for what it is . . . a global centre of mental ill-health. President George W. Bush was keen to impress when he told the world, 'The problem with the French is they have no word for entrepreneur.' Never mind his stupidity; this is not a criticism he could have levelled at London, because the place has too many words for entrepreneur.

The Roman root of the word London means 'place at the unfordable river'. Thanks to a series of governments who have known the price of everything but the value of nothing, the metropolis has since become the *unaffordable place on the river*. Financiers, property developers and buy-to-let opportunists have been unmuzzled, creating an environment in which most people have to frantically run the gerbil wheel just to survive – and if you look closely you'll see the wheel is distorting under its own centrifugal force. Soon it's going to fly apart.

One morning on my bicycle commute through the traffic jams of the Square Mile I find my way blocked by two high-ranking gerbils in expensive suits. They are standing on a central island, waiting to cross the road. My route would take me right past them, except part of their anatomy is blocking the narrow gap in the traffic – their massive stomachs cantilevered out into the Queen's highway. Not that I have any choice, I stop, and can't help but laugh at this beautiful metaphor.

Rather than having a problem with bloated stomachs, the ninety-four people who kill themselves during the average week in Britain are clearly sick to the pit of their stomachs. And in London, suicide by drowning in the Thames is not uncommon. But as well as the suicides, lifeboat crews are kept busy by other folks whose survival strategy is to get totally pissed and/or take narcotics, and in this intoxicated state they end up in the cold, dangerous waters of the Thames. Perhaps a swim just seemed like a good idea. Some survive, some don't.

The taking of mind-altering chemicals has become so common that the very river water these people immerse themselves in is itself a cocktail of the drugs they have taken. Research shows that cocaine in human urine, which finds its way into the Thames via the sewage system, is adversely affecting fish. I need to get away from this mental mayhem, to move out of this dirty old town, before I too become a statistic.

***

Unexpressed emotions will never die. They are buried alive and will come forth later in uglier ways.

SIGMUND FREUD

A few years ago my friend Harry was given the all-clear from lung cancer. She had a rough ride, enduring the foul effects of chemotherapy and the threat of imminent death. During that time she remained honest and brave. For much of her life she has struggled with suicidal feelings, and we often talk about psychological survival in a culture which makes mental wellbeing a challenge. The work she has done on herself is evident in her authenticity and I always look forward to our conversations.

Perhaps it happened while I was with Harry because subconsciously I felt safe in her company, that I knew she wouldn't judge me. Granted, I hadn't been feeling on top form but I wasn't expecting to suddenly collapse and fall to the floor with a hysterical panic attack. The dam holding back the floodwaters of my repressed emotions burst. I was laid bare. My vulnerability clear to see. I was right, if anything Harry and I are better friends after my mental melt down.

The artist Yayoi Kusama has an obsession with obliteration, which she represents through the polka-dotting of people, objects and canvases. Of course she's right: we're all eventually obliterated, and not only by death. In life our individuality is also obliterated by the requirements of the System. And if that weren't enough, we are all obliterated by our own insignificance in the universe. Yet for me these existential obliterations are easier to cope with than the issue of obliteration by shit.

Shit happens. Sooner or later we pass within range of life's shit-throwing fan: we get sacked, our significant other leaves us, loved ones go mad and or die. You can't avoid being polka-dotted by it, and as time passes, unless you take care of your mental hygiene, eventually you may go mad yourself.

RESILIENCE

Bureaucracies force us to practice nonsense. And if you rehearse non-sense, you may one day find yourself the victim of it.

LAWRENCE GONZALES

I'd been wondering if was experiencing a midlife crisis. But the truth is I've been depressed most of my life, and my life is past its mid point, so to call it such would be inaccurate.

The breakdown which started in Harry's flat left me feeling embarrassed and useless. I was a wreck. Friends advised me to get help, so I referred myself to Hackney's mental health team. I was given an appointment for a telephone consultation, during which a voice asked many personal questions, then got round to, *Do you feel suicidal?* and *do you I want to be alive?* My replies – *no* and *no.*

What with my poor track record with institutions, I wasn't feeling comfortable about letting these mental health technocrats into my life. Paranoid? Certainly. My concern was that they could use this information against me, or make me look like an idiot. Or both. And sure enough, I got the feeling the guy on the phone could just as well have been working on a telephone help-line, troubleshooting a problem with a washing machine.

His final question was about drug and alcohol use. When I told him how much I was drinking I was informed I should to refer myself to a drug and alcohol unit. The transition from 'consult-ation' to that click as he hung up left me feeling hurt, angry and abandoned. I wondered if he was keen to get onto the next call from a hot chick with a wool programme problem.

I stared at the disconnected phone and noticed my knuckles had gone white where I was squeezing it so hard. I had an urge to throw myself to the floor sobbing, then anger welled up, and for a second I considered flinging the phone against the wall while screaming 'fucking bastards', but my manliness programming overrode the crying option, while the expense and inconvenience of destroying the phone overcame my fury. What actually happened was that the dagger of unexpressed emotion twisted in my guts.

***

Institutions. Am I imagining it, or do they attract mindlessness like a fishing boat attracts seagulls? I ask myself if I'm being reasonable with such thoughts, or if I've locked myself into a mindset of negativity. Well, it appears the wearing of poo-tinted spectacles is normal: all emotions are not created equal. According to social scientists humans are hardwired with 'negativity bias'. Research reveals that negative or unpleasant information and experiences are more influential to people's decision making than positive ones. It's this trait which is exploited by politicians who would rather slag off their opponents than promote their own ideas, if they have any.

Whatever team Hackney's mental health team are on, it isn't mine. Thinking about the guy on the phone, I wondered, 'Did he care how shit that made me feel?' I suspect he couldn't have cared less. He'd been allocated a batch of phone numbers. Mine was one of them. Just another nutter he was paid to talk to before lunch. His role, to read questions designed by someone else, to elicit binary answers. Did I feel like killing myself? Yes or no. He'd check the appropriate box on a computer screen, and at end of the session an algorithm would instruct him what to say next.

He'd been disabused of any autonomy in his job. The guy's working on a mental health production line.

Wondering where he'd turn if his own life was falling apart, I realised that he and I are on the same team after all – *Team Keep it Together in Difficult Times.*

Bollocks to Hackney's *Mental* Health Team, I'm going to keep on swimming and writing. The swimming is where I go to maintain sanity, the writing is where I become a crash scene investigator sifting through the wreckage of my life.

***

The oak fought the wind and was broken, the willow bent when it must and survived.

ROBERT JORDAN, from *The Fires of Heaven*

By not throwing myself sobbing to the ground or flinging the phone against the wall, I was demonstrating resilience. That's a good thing, right? The social commentator Farrah Jarral notes that historically the word resilience was first used to describe the robustness and reliability of machines and structures. Today it's used to describe the human ability to hold ground against misfortune. It's entirely consistent with the logic of a free-market industrial society that an attribute desirable in machines should be apportioned to flesh and blood; after all, in the workplace we are often treated as though we were machines. And indeed we only have a job until they invent a machine that can do it cheaper.

Jarral views this cultural notion of resilience as a mechanism by which the structural failings of our society are allowed to persist in what she terms the *resilience circus.* Well, I feel like a drunken clown in that circus, and it looks like there are plenty of other people who feel the same.

As well as disaster in our personal lives there is always the danger of society-wide crisis: conflict, pandemic, economic crash. Our reserves of resilience need to be ready for such things, not depleted in a battle for day-to-day survival caused by the way our economy and society are managed. After all, we wouldn't snack on a life-raft's emergency rations when there's no emergency.

We may bend like the willow in a gale, but if the tree is already weakened by previous storms it may fall.

EUPHORIC

Ridicule is the best test of truth.

LORD CHESTERFIELD

A monthly pass for London Fields Lido has been facilitating daily swims, which continue to keep my head above water emotionally. The drinking however hasn't diminished and, drunk at a party – again – my friend Stef and I get into conversation with a guy who has butterflied (swimming stroke) the English Channel (in a relay team). He persuades us to enter a short race at his swim club at the Serpentine, the lake in the middle of London's Hyde Park.

It's a Saturday in midwinter. The parked cars are covered in frost, and the early morning cycle ride across London is freezing. It's a mere forty-metre swim, how hard can it be? The handsome half-Lebanese, half-Australian Stef does well, and certainly doesn't disgrace himself. Unlike me. Having failed to take account of the fact I wouldn't be able to control my breathing because of the cold, I stop halfway in a fit of coughing and limp over the line last, only to be informed by an official that I'm disqualified because I'm wearing neoprene gloves.

Hey, I came last, who cares about the gloves, I think. However it appears the Serpentine Swimming Club has a grudge against neoprene; the self-appointed neoprene policewoman is clearly enjoying ridiculing me, and who am I to spoil her fun. But in any case I couldn't care less about being humiliated, because the cold water has washed away a layer of mental shit. I'm feeling euphoric.

***

Those who live by the sea can hardly form a single thought of which the sea would not be part.

HERMANN BROCH

The collective psychosis of the metropolis pushes me out and away from London, while at the same time the sea and welcoming friends pull me towards the coast and Brighton. I've been spending most weekends there, a situation which has grown into a long-term plan to move to the seaside.

Brighton isn't a city in its own right. Brighton and Hove *are . . .* or should that be *is*? Having one place with two names is confusing, but as they grew and merged, it must have made sense to slip in an *and* and have one administration for both towns, and for them to become one city with two names.

Like many seaside towns the light in Brighton and Hove is sharp, the air clean and the social atmosphere relaxed. In so many ways it's the opposite of the capital. The average Brightonian spends more in coffee shops than in any other place in the country. The frequency of comedy business names are a sign of the settlement's good humour. A hairdressers called Off Yer Head. A plumbers called U Benders. A removal company whose name mixes superheroes, He Van: Movers of the Universe, a tree surgeon called Arbor Barbers, and many others. Brighton's environmental credentials are bolstered by having the nation's only Green MP. Have you ever noticed that many words have significant sub words within them? Brighton – bright and right-on. The name is appropriate.

However, like London, Brighton and Hove's property prices are outlandish, a situation which fuels inequality and spiralling levels of homelessness. Such political issues bother me. Politics – that's another interesting word. In the phonetic sense – poly meaning many, and tics meaning blood-sucking parasites.

My yearning to be near the sea continues to grow, not only because it's uplifting to look at but also because I want to experiment with swimming in it on a regular basis. That's why I've made contact with the Hove Sea Swimmers.

Most of them don't bother with wetsuits, even in midwinter. My first swim with them was in a wetsuit, but even covered in its insulating layer I was frozen after twenty minutes. I was curious: how could these people swim in such cold water without a wetsuit? A couple of weeks later I decided to find out.

I was nervous. James, a man who is completely indifferent to cold and never so much as shivers, offered to swim with me on my maiden winter 'skin' sea swim. 'Yes please,' I blurted.

The sea temperature was 11 °C. 'This is only unpleasantness – it will pass,' I kidded myself. Actually it was pain. An all-over aching, morphing into a burning sensation. Even wearing a swim cap I had a serious case of ice-cream head. There was a strong urge to swim for shore, run up the beach, dress as quickly as possible, and never do this again. But my life felt like a bag of shite and this was an experiment with making it better. After a couple of minutes the intensity of the pain subsided. James stuck close by, giving me the confidence to stay in for ten minutes.

Back on the beach I was shivering so intensely it was difficult to dress, and when I tried to pour a cup of tea from the thermos half of it slopped out of the cup. It didn't bother me at all. I may have been cold, but like after the Serpentine swim I felt euphoric. The depression had entirely vanished.

STRAPLINES

There are wounds that never show on the body that are deeper and more hurtful than anything that bleeds.

LAURELL K. HAMILTON

I've come up with the – possibly stupid – idea of swimming across the Thames. After inspecting the map and bicycling both banks, I see it would, in theory, be possible to swim from Creekmouth in east London, on the north side of the river, to Margaret Ness, a promontory on the south side. But according to the Port of London Authority (PLA), 'you encounter a fast running tide, bridges and eddies which can drag a person underwater in a trice. And there are also passenger vessels which carry over six million people a year and 1,000 tonne barges carrying freight.'

The PLA go on to say swimming in the Thames is about as sensible as wandering about on the M25. Which is why swimming in the Thames is banned.

In a colour choice which grossly misrepresents reality, my old paper *A to Z* shows the Thames in light blue. On it I measure fifty-five millimetres of blue ink, which scales up to a kilometre across a stretch of river known as Gallions Reach. On the north side of Gallions Reach, the River Rodding debouches into the Thames. At this meeting place of rivers is Beckton Sewage Works. East of the Rodding is the potholed River Road, and an industrial area hosting waste recycling, scrap metal processing and other unglamorous but necessary activities.

On the south side is Thamesmead, a deprived neighbourhood of council estates. The area is also home to three centres of incarceration: HMP Belmarsh, HMP Thameside, and a young offenders' institute, HMP Isis. My previous experience of the locality comes from my appearance on the guest list of Tameside Prison, when for obvious reasons I didn't get to know the locality. I can tell you about the jail though. It's run by SERCO, whose corporate strapline is *bringing service to life.*

Have you ever noticed how straplines usually represent the opposite of an organisation's actual values? Their jail stank of men and depression, and not long after my release the place was put on a 24-hour lockdown because violence was spiralling out of control. But the thing that really got to me was the fact that SERCO turn a profit charging prisoners premium rates to phone out of their evil-smelling shit hole. On arrest I'd had a wallet full of cash which was transferred to an account which I used up entirely on phone calls. Other prisoners were less fortunate, consequently their families had no idea where they were until several weeks after their arrest.

***

Gallions Reach may be in the metropolis yet it's a forgotten place, an uncared for, unseen, timeless zone most Londoners have never heard of. Only the gulls and the fish high on cocaine really know the place. It has an end of the world feel – and for many the place has been the end.

It's 3 September 1878, and Captain Grinstead is about to navigate his pretty 250-ton paddle steamer, the *Princess Alice*, through Gallions Reach on its return passage to Woolwich Pier. A couple of hours ago he stood on the ship's bridge watching some seven hundred happy Londoners return to his vessel after a day trip to Rosherville Pleasure Gardens in Gravesend.

It's just before eight on a gorgeous summer evening. The sun has already set, but the sky to the west is still bright. The night will never fall into complete darkness because of the full moon. On the crowded deck there's a party atmosphere, a band plays and people are singing and dancing. Courting couples cuddle, families chat about the day, and tired children sleep in the arms of their parents. It has been a magical day.

The smell of sewage is in the air, its source the Northern Outfall sewage pipe which is currently discharging. But this doesn't bother Londoners of the 1800s, who are used to the fetid odours of the metropolis.

The *Bywell Castle* was built to carry coal, and is made of iron, a much heavier and stronger vessel than the *Princess Alice*. Just out of dry dock for maintenance, she's making her way in the opposite direction out of London. Amongst those on the ship's bridge are Captain Harrison and a pilot who, if things go to plan, will guide the vessel out of the Thames Estuary.

Down in the *Alice*'s boiler-room the stokers are working up a sweat shovelling coal into the firebox. Her engine is working hard, pushing the overloaded ship against the ebbing tide. Her twin paddles make a rhythmic sound, sending a soothing vibration through her white hull. In her wake she leaves two stripes of cream-coloured froth.

The rule of sea and rivers is that vessels pass to starboard of each other, but for the *Alice* following this convention would mean taking a longer line around Margaret Ness, and because she is battling the current Captain Grinstead orders the coxswain to steer to port, crossing in front of the *Bywell Castle*.

On the bridge of both vessels there must have been a heart-stopping moment when both captains knew they'd made an error.

A witness report tells how Captain Grinstead on the *Alice* made the futile gesture of shouting up at the *Bywell Castle*, 'Good God, where are you coming to?'

The *Bywell Castle*'s iron bow ploughs into the lighter ship's side. There's a sickening crashing sound, then the splintering and cracking of wooden planks, the grinding of metal, and the screaming of terrified people. The initial motion aboard the *Alice* is violent; most of those on deck are immediately thrown overboard. The paddle steamer is broken in two and sinks within minutes. Those trapped below deck have no chance, while those above are left to the mercy of the Thames and its ferocious current.

For fully clothed people who couldn't swim their only hope was to cling to the floating debris. What should have been a happy end to a beautiful day ended in carnage. Within minutes hundreds were drowned in the disgusting sewage-filled water. The coroner's report contains the witness account of Miss Emma Eatwell of 32 Half Moon Street, London:

The band was playing at the time, they had been playing We Don't Want to Fight and then they had been playing a polka, and as I pushed past there were three or four girls trying to dance to it but there was not room. There was a certain amount of joviality and confusion which drew my attention off – I was saved after being in the water for half an hour . . . I could see all the poor souls struggling in the water. I suffered very much from the state of the water and my chest is now very bad. The water was very dreadful and nasty – it was in a very foul state indeed.

More than sixty people were saved, but some 650 died. The exact numbers are unknown because there was no accurate passenger manifest. Apart from a few scratches to her new paintwork, the *Bywell Castle* was undamaged. Emma Eatwell's lungs may have been badly affected by the filthy water, but I wonder about her emotional state. Being surrounded by drowning people, the trauma of the disaster would most likely have burned itself into her psyche, perhaps leaving her with survivor's guilt.

The terrible scene viewed from above on the *Bywell Castle* must have replayed over and over again in Captain Harrison's mind, which would explain why, even though officially cleared of responsibility, he never put to sea again. Captain Grinstead did not survive.

* * *

Trauma affects many of us. It could be a medical intervention, or some random event such as an accident. Psychologists believe trauma can be trapped not only within a person's psyche but also in their body, creating negative feedback loops of learned helplessness, anger, aggression, drug dependency and alcoholism.

Events in my life have left their footprints in my character. A near drowning stayed with me for years in the form of flashbacks and nightmares. The physical pain and the sudden immobility caused by arthritis in many of my joints, which left me barely able to walk, obliterated my self-confidence and left me feeling helpless. The experience of nearly being killed by the drugs I was given to treat the illness added to the horror. I count myself lucky I survived the drugs and that the arthritis gradually faded away. But though my physical body recovered, my soul hasn't.

Amongst other mishaps I still carry vivid images from an ultimately pointless rescue attempt of two pilots whose light aircraft collided and crash-landed on mudflats on the banks of the River Hamble. But the experience I feel most negatively impacted by is my six years at primary school where I learned absolutely nothing, but during which I was humiliated on a minute-by-minute basis and bullied by an abusive headmaster.

I'm tired of carrying this psychic baggage, it's too heavy. The upshot of an unresolved past is that I feel about as competent a captain of my own soul as Captains Grinstead and Harrison were of their vessels.

* * *

Almost a century and a half after the *Princess Alice* disaster I stand on the north bank of the Thames looking out over Gallions Reach. In the middle of the river I can see an eddy fence, the interface between water flowing in different directions, probably caused by the bend in the river. On it are pieces of driftwood going round and round in circles. Not exactly whirlpools, but almost. The water looks chaotic, dangerous and unpredictable. I realise that if the swim is possible it will have to be done on a neap tide at slack water.

***

Ships don't sink because of the water around them; ships sink because of the water that gets in them.

UNKNOWN

Most people I know who live on boats have occasional nightmares about sinking. This isn't paranoia. I have two friends whose boats sank. For one it happened while he was asleep. He was woken when the water reached his bed. Luckily he got out before the boat went down. But he was extremely upset about losing his vinyl record collection, which to this day lies within his wrecked boat on the bottom of the River Lea in Hackney. The other friend returned home drunk after a night out to find just his boat's chimney sticking out of the water.

So, one night when I woke in the early hours to find my bed soaking, I feared the worst. My barely conscious mind was trying to process why my bed was wet, as were my pants and T-shirt. It didn't take long to figure out that it had nothing to do with sinking, but everything to do with having gone to bed rolling drunk. I'd wet my own bed for the first time since childhood.

It's not my boat that's sinking, it's me.

MISTAKES

My story starts at sea . . . a perilous voyage to an unknown land . . . a shipwreck . . . The wild waters roar and heave . . . The brave vessel is dashed all to pieces, and all the helpless souls within her drowned . . . all save one . . . a lady . . . whose soul is greater than the ocean . . . and her spirit stronger than the sea's embrace . . . Not for her a watery end, but a new life beginning on a stranger shore. It will be a love story . . . for she will be my heroine for all time. And her name will be . . . Viola.

WILLIAM SHAKESPEARE

While in Devon visiting my dad I'm invited to a book launch for *Wild Swimming Walks: Dartmoor and South Devon* by Matt Newbury and Sophie Pierce. The event consists of a walk and two swims taken from the book, at Compass Cove and Sugary Cove.

Toponymy, the study of place names, may have its experts but my research on the names of Compass and Sugary Coves is a dead end. Their names, though, suggest a connection with shipwrecks. And this rocky coastline with its unpredictable weather and strong currents has claimed ships carrying everything from Islamic gold and silver to coal and china clay.

The sea, shipwrecks, and mistakes have become an ongoing theme in my life. Mistakes at sea can so easily end badly, and the fact that otherwise competent captains fuck up helps me look more kindly on the catalogue of errors that is my own life.

I meet a bunch of swimmers and literary folks in a car park

west of Dartmouth. From there we set off on foot east along the coast path high up on the cliff tops, with the sea to our right and fields to the left. A couple of miles distant, set upon a sparkling sea, two small granite islands give the view a sense of geological time. After a mile we descend steep zigzagging wooden steps into the small, south-facing, boulder-strewn Compass Cove. The remnant of a large electrical cable, its fraying end spewing smaller cables, emerges from the ground at the back of the beach. According to *Wild Swimming Walks* this is the remains of a telegraph cable laid in 1884, connecting mainland Britain to the island of Guernsey. It was apparently severed, along with a lot of other things, during the Second World War.

The sun may be out, but the air temperature is low and the sea cold. I stay in for perhaps ten minutes, hoping I've left enough body heat for a second swim. Comparing myself to other sea swimmers I have a low resistance to cold, but that isn't important to me. This isn't a competition – rather it's a means of mental survival.

We climb back out of the cove and continue east towards the mouth of the River Dart, then walk inland high on the river's steep western shoreline. On the way I get into a conversation with another swimmer who tells me she has driven 18,000 miles over the previous year visiting different swimming locations around the country, a testament to how addictive swimming is for some. We make another descent, into the southeast-facing Sugary Cove. Its beach, some thirty metres wide, is enclosed on three sides by craggy rock faces. I haven't warmed up, but get in anyhow. The water is crystal clear. I swim through a rock archway – another first for me.

* * *

Dalmatians are not only superior to other dogs, they are like all dogs, infinitely less stupid than men.

EUGENE O'NEILL

Back in London for a doctor's appointment. 'Too much heavy lifting,' she tells me I have two hernias which will require an operation. After years of heavy manual work on building sites I guess this shouldn't be a surprise. I was chucked out of school at 16, then went to six form collage from where I was also chucked out after a few months for, amongst other things, riding my moped down a collage corridor. So I applied to join the navy, but perhaps the recruiting sergeant could see this crazy mixed up kit might just point the gun at himself or a commanding officer as at the people he was ordered to kill. So when people ask me if I was ever in the military my answer is 'no I did something far more dangerous . . . working on building sites in the 1970s'. Near misses included. . . a fall in a lift shaft and nearly being crushed by machines, so I guess I should count myself lucky I got away with mere hernias.

Now I'm back in the capital, my mood has sunk. Some say Winston Churchill was a depressive and that he described his depression as his *Black Dog*. While I like the idea of a term which is less stigmatising I don't subscribe to the notion that all things black are bad so I call my depressive states my Grey Hound. And right now the Grey Mutt has its canine teeth sunk into my mental flesh. I've learned that I can often prevent a surface wound turning into a serious mauling by activity, so I hatch a plan to visit Peacehaven, a small coastal settlement a few miles east of Brighton.

Peacehaven is a quiet, friendly, unostentatious town with a flavour of eccentricity. There are no old buildings here for a reason. I wonder what it would be like to go back in time, to when the place was full of people living in makeshift shacks and second-hand buildings bought from a nearby military base. I can imagine people socialising round open fires in the summer months, living a good life on the cheap. Many of those early residents would have experienced the horrors and trauma of trench warfare.

Land for the town was acquired by the entrepreneur Charles Neville in 1916. His idea was to profit from selling cheap plots of land on which people could build their own homes. He marketed the plan with a competition in the *Daily Express* newspaper to name the town. It was won by Ethel Radford from Leicestershire. The winner and runners-up, he claimed, would receive the prize of a free plot of land. Except they weren't entirely free; competition winners still had to pay legal fees for transferring the ownership of their plots. The *Express* sued Neville for false advertising; they won the case, but the publicity gave Neville's project a boost and he sold all the plots. He went on to build the nearby town of Saltdean and was a key player in the development of Rottingdean.

It's easy to see why the name Peacehaven was attractive in Britain in 1917. Though the end of the First World War was in sight, its brutality and attrition had wounded the nation's collective psyche. Yet the place name would prove to be more hopeful than realistic, because only two years later a cruel pandemic of flu would sweep across the world, and a couple of decades after that a bunch of German sociopaths would bring the world into a state of chaos and conflict yet again.

Peacehaven may have an unusual history, but this isn't its main attraction to me. The draw is to swim under its white chalk cliffs.

It's a warm sunny day, perfect for motorcycling from London to Brighton, where I'm to meet Nicky, a new friend from the Hove

Sea-Swimming Group. Whatever I love doing, the Grey Hound hates in equal measure; this time it's the motorbike ride along the coast road with views over the South Downs and across the green sparkling sea of the English Channel. As we travel I can feel the dog's grip on my psyche loosening.

We park up on the accurately named Cliff Avenue and descend via some steps a hundred and fifty feet to sea level, arriving on a concrete walkway built to prevent the sea eroding the cliffs. If left undefended the average chalk cliff will erode at the rate of forty centimetres a year.

It's high tide and incoming waves are bouncing back off the sea wall. Where the incoming and outgoing waves meet there are huge steep-sided mountains of water which last only a second, leaving behind equally deep troughs. Nicky and I are discussing the likelihood of dangerous currents when an older guy with an open shirt, a towel round his neck, walks past. We ask him about the currents. He swims most days on his own, but stays close to shore because he has a dicky heart. He assures us there are no dangerous currents. We decide to take the plunge.

A hundred metres out we turn east, swimming parallel with the shore. Even out here the sea is chaotic, making swimming hard work and progress slow. The sunlight reflecting off the white cliffs is intense. Swimming under the them makes me think of a recent cliff fall a few miles east, when thousands of tonnes of chalk fell into the sea without warning – an event remarkably caught on camera.

Evidence of chalk eroding from the seabed is in the water, which is cream coloured up to about 100 metres out, where it abruptly changes back to its natural green. The chalky water is a good 3 °C warmer; just a couple of metres across the boundary into the green there's a sudden drop in temperature. Given the surface turbulence it's surprising the water isn't mixing. A small demonstration of how difficult it is to predict the sea. We swim past the end of the sea defences, where up above the town of Peacehaven also ends, and make landfall on a small shingle beach, not lingering because of the danger of a cliff fall. The swim back is equally labour intensive.

Back on dry land we sit on the edge of the walkway, eating our packed lunch. A dog walker passes by with an unusually muscular Dalmatian. Though disappointed we won't share our sandwiches, the creature is all wagging tail. I realise this is exactly like me. My mood has gone from Grey Hound to tail-wagging black and white spotty dog without a trace of depression.

After the swim we ride around Peacehaven's back streets looking for evidence of the original structures. We find none. They must have rotted away long ago. Today the town's housing consists, in the main, of ordinary-looking bungalows.

The settlement's connection with the right-leaning *Daily Express* perhaps explains its Conservative politics today. But the town has the feel of a libertarian right rather than an authoritarian one, perhaps the legacy of a town built by its own inhabitants. I can't help wondering if this isn't a model for solving today's housing crisis. Small cheap plots of land on which people can build their own homes.

CRAPPER

Sure, we need the gypsies, we always have. Because if you don't have someone to run out of town once in a while, how are you going to know you yourself belong there?

STEPHEN KING, *Thinner*

As swimming will be on the menu, I can't say no when an old friend invites me to stay in a yurt in Cornwall. And on the way I can visit Harry, who is in Devon on a year-long meditation retreat. I guess that makes her a kind of temporary nun. Harry and I rendezvous on a quiet country lane, and the nun and I take off on the motorbike headed for Dornafield campsite where my tent is pitched.

Numerous signs dotted about Dornafield inform visitors that the campsite has won Toilet of the Year, many years running. Clean would be an understatement. Total war has been declared on germs, and with Radio Devon playing 24/7 to drown out any embarrassing lavatorial noise, Thomas Crapper would have been proud.

At Dornafield an old orchard is put aside for people like me, who are sleeping under canvas. The rest of the place is for those under the tin roofs of campers and caravans, some the size of buses; gleaming rows of them remind me of a domestic appliance shop, and like washing machines they all have electrical and water hook-ups. These part-time gypsies aren't slumming it. Their affluence is evident from the value of their well-equipped homes from home, many with gleaming ensuite 4x4.

After breakfast and use of the Toilet of the Year we set off for Teignmouth and the beach, riding down lanes overhanging with verdant summer vegetation. By the time we arrive the cause of that lush flora is falling from the sky. The air and sea are cold. The idea of swimming is met with a a complete refusal from Harry so I swim alone. After twenty minutes in the murky water I come out shivering, but with the usual mood uplift.

If you're a bilateral breather in front crawl, the stroke is centred around an in-breath every three strokes, which gives it the rhythm of a waltz. In meditation the breath is used as a harmless distraction from our usual round of random thoughts, worries and anxieties. Harry is an experienced meditator and believes the rhythm of breathing in swimming gives it a meditative quality. Perhaps that's why it can have such a positive effect on one's mood.

***

The next day I load the motorbike and head west for the tiny Cornish village of Gorran. My first thought is that this will be the furthest west I've been in Britain, but then I remember that the westernmost point of mainland Britain is in Scotland, where I was last winter working on a film, sleeping in a leaking tent in the rain on a beach near the settlement of Acharacle in Argyll.
Cotna Eco Yurt is not a contender for Toilet of the Year – it doesn't actually have a toilet as most people would know it. The facilities consist of a shed on stilts, built over a pile of poo. Instead of a flush you grab a handful of sawdust and chuck it on top of your contribution. There's no radio to disguise lavatorial noise; instead there's the clucking of free range chickens, the quack of ducks, and the sound of horses' rubber-lipped exhalations. There is something beautiful about seeing animals silhouetted on the ridge of a hill – and so it is with the horses, cows and sheep at Cotna.

The owners of Dornafield and Cotna both bought small farms of around seventeen acres, both on hilly ground and unprofitable for traditional farming. Both enterprises have turned to the farming of tourists, but with entirely different philosophies. Cotna has three yurts, an apartment to rent, and sells wholemeal bread and freshly picked vegetables. Dornafield has over a hundred pitches, wireless access, and a well-stocked shop. At Dornafield chemical war is waged on germs, while at Cotna an alliance has been made with them.

* * *

A yurt is a round tent which might better be called a small marquee. Its floor plan is circular, with vertical walls up to shoulder height. A conical roof comes to a peak in the centre of the structure, giving plenty of headroom. They've been used for centuries by the nomadic peoples of central Asia, of whom there are a lot fewer than there used to be for two main reasons: persecution and climate change.

Stalin, the paranoid vodka-guzzling despot, exterminated and resettled the yurt-dwellers of the Soviet Union. The only country where the lifestyle is still practised is Mongolia. However, the severity of recent winters, for which climate change has been blamed, has devastated the nomads' livestock, forcing many to pitch their yurts permanently on the outskirts of Mongolia's capital, Ulaanbaatar. I can relate to their loss, going from the freedom to roam, hunt and tend their animals on the wide open steppe to being thrust into the cash economy, forced into running the gerbil wheel.

While the number of people living a nomadic lifestyle is decreasing on the Mongolian steppe, so it is increasing in London. The housing crisis has spawned a huge growth in the number of people living on boats. The authorities require boat dwellers like me without a home mooring to move their boats every two weeks. Their stupid regulations have thus created a whole tribe of modern-day urban nomads.

A constant in human affairs is that gypsies and people living different lifestyles are perceived as a threat by the population and institutions of mainstream society. The Canal and River Trust (CRT), who manage the waterways I live on, are no exception. Unlike Stalin they don't have the power to exterminate us; their approach is instead to force us to move every fourteen days, to make our lives as difficult as possible. Non-compliance leads to the seizure and destruction of people's homes. The boat dwellers who fall foul of their hostility are usually folks with mental or physical health problems.

Unlike the nomads of the steppe, who move in accord with the needs of their herds and in cohesive community groups, live-aboard boaters in the metropolis move mostly to comply with the logic of a hostile bureaucracy. This has the effect of atomising community, a situation I have always found unsettling. But our temporary yurt home at Cotna hasn't moved for years and I'm happy to spend a week in this comfortable dwelling.

The closest hamlet to Cotna is Mevagissey, a commercial fishing port. Its beauty attracts people from places like London who are keen to acquire second homes in the village; the upshot is that locals are priced out, a cause of much resentment. Similar to us boat dwellers who have been priced out of living on land in London.

Mevagissey's emerald-green water is almost the same colour as the grey seal we find in its harbour. Judging by its enormous bulk it's probably a male, perhaps weighing in at around 300kg, with long eyebrows and the expressive face of a sweet-looking dog. Considering his bulk he's timid. But you trust humans at your peril. One minute they'll smile and give you fish, the next they'll harpoon you in the back and club your pups to death.

You're spoilt for choice with beaches in Cornwall, and during school term-time they aren't busy. I swim at Porthpean, Vault and Hemmick Beaches. We arrive at Porthpean in the early evening and take the motorbike right down to the beach. We are the only people there. Though the air is warm the sea is cold. The beach is around three hundred metres wide with yellowy/cream coloured sand which slopes gently. The bay is backed by low cliffs topped with pine trees. It feels intimate and safe.

Vault Beach is bigger; lying in the lea of Dodman Point, it will have calm water most of the time. A mixture of light grey sand and shingle, it can only be accessed on foot along a rough footpath. This beach is also empty except for one other group of tourists, and there are no other swimmers. Hemmick Beach faces southwest and so cops the full force of the prevailing wind and waves. Golden sand and lots of craggy rock pools at low tide. All these beaches are on the south coast and because there are northerly winds while we're in Cornwall the sea is flat. Being on a peninsula has the advantage that you will almost always be able to find calm water, no matter what the wind strength and direction.

My experience of sea swimming is limited, mostly to the English Channel. A result of which is that I'm accustomed to swimming in murky water. The crystal-clear water of Cornwall makes me nervous, because in it you can see life. Most of the time that life consists of seaweed, but it's evidence that you are immersed in a completely untamed environment, with no barriers between you and all the other life forms in it. Some of which have teeth and poisonous tentacles.

HERMITS

Many times a day I realise how much my own outer and inner life is built upon the labours of my fellow men, both living and dead, and how earnestly I must exert myself in order to give in return as much as I have received.

ALBERT EINSTEIN

I leave Cornwall in the early hours on the motorbike heading for Yorkshire to see my mum. She has just gone blind and been diagnosed with Parkinson's disease. It's going to be a long ride on the uncomfortable old machine.

The next day, in the car park of Mum's rest home, I notice a skip. It's full of the belongings of a recently deceased resident. A book stares out at me, *Mastering Calligraphy*. I wonder if the book's owner ever fulfilled that intention. I think of the books on my shelves. When I die will I have *Overcome Depression*, or found *Personal Reconciliation*?

Seeing family dredges up the depression I felt as a child, which makes me wonder if I've progressed at all. I think of a conversation Harry and I had in Devon about all things being transitory. Not so with depression, which has been a constant companion in my life.

Here in Leeds my options for swimming venues are limited by the fact that I have no transport – the elderly motorbike has suffered a catastrophic mechanical failure and is at the menders. Unlike my mum it will soon be back on the road, but in the meantime I'm forced into walking and jogging. I discover Leeds has a network of footpaths, and cut-throughs, known locally as ginnels. I witness only a handful of dog walkers using them, but it's clear they were used extensively in the past. In one ginnel I notice a flight of steps on which there has been sufficient footfall to wear two inches of stone from their upper surface. Looking closer I discover that the underside of the stone slabs has also worn to the same extent. Many years ago they must have been turned over to provide a fresh unworn surface, which has itself been worn down. This amount of wear would have taken many feet many years, which is plausible because the steps lead down to the site of the now ruined Kirkstall Abbey, which was founded in 1152.

***

These worn steps are visible evidence of the ancestors, of their vitality and numbers. I imagine a time when this ginnel was a busy thoroughfare. Friends greet each other, people stop and chat. I see feet, wealthy ones in shoes, poor ones in clogs or barefoot, skin on stone. Young people bounding up and down making light work of gravity, while elders are slowed by the effects of time on flesh. Ponies trudge up and down loaded with goods.

Before it was an abbey the site was home to hermits. At the time of its construction the abbey was what we might now call a development scheme. History records that some of the hermits were paid to leave, while others decided to join the monks at the new religious institution.

Progress frequently involves casualties, and the hermits were collateral damage in someone else's grand project. I'm an expert in the field of grand project collateral damage because my home, our homes and community, stood in the way of the great steamroller that was the London Olympics.

***

Home was then the Clays Lane Housing Cooperative, in Stratford, East London, where five hundred of us lived. A kind of village within a city. We had a sign near the entrance to our land. It said *Shelter, Friendship, Community*. We lost the co-op because we were legally outmanoeuvred, along with a lot of other people and businesses who were occupying land wanted for the Olympic Park.

As we were evicted from our homes, men with sledgehammers were sent in with orders to smash the inside of our houses to make absolutely sure no one could move in after we moved out. Windows and doors were then covered with metal grilles. Eventually, after they had smashed and grilled all our homes, they demolished them altogether, leaving mounds of rubble. The mounds were then ground up into nugget-sized lumps which were left in slightly smaller heaps. Eventually the heaps and all traces of our houses vanished.

A few years earlier I had stood in the kitchen of our house voicing the opinion to friends and neighbours that the land our cooperative stood on had become too valuable, and that someone would try and take the place from us. No one took me seriously. Now, a few years on, and the chair of the co-op was found dead and decomposed in his flat in suspicious circumstances, our homes destroyed and our bank account plundered to the tune of £800,000.

The fun times, the warmth, shelter and friendship, the sense of community, the place called home had been erased. All my life I'd struggled to find a place where I felt I belonged. This had been it. Whenever I think of its destruction I can feel the tears welling up – but being a man, and being resilient, I don't let them out.

People have an emotional attachment to places, particularly if that place is home. Which is why moving them requires the application of force and/or bribery. I'd love to go back in time and ask the hermits how they felt about their homes being taken by the builders of the abbey.

During their four centuries at the site the industrious Cistercian monks of Kirkstall became world leaders in metallurgy, making an important contribution to the emerging industrial revolution. But then, in 1539, it was the abbey's turn for destruction in Henry VIII's Dissolution of the Monasteries. After the dissolution of the abbey the site became known as Kirkstall Forge and continued as an important centre of industry, linked to the rest of the country first by canal, then rail. For many centuries Kirkstall employed thousands of people, their toing and froing no doubt contributing to the wear in the stone steps, until the contraction of manufacturing in Britain from the 1980s led to the closure of the Kirkstall Industrial Centre. The land then stood empty for a few decades. But with the River Aire running adjacent, you wouldn't get many points for guessing whose snouts are now in the trough.

Hoardings covered with glossy images depicting the imaginary lifestyle of its residents surround the development of yet more steel-framed buildings with balconies overlooking a waterway. Someone in the developer's marketing team probably got a promotion for thinking up a new word which is plastered all over the hoardings – *unsuburbia*. A reference to the site's location within woods and parkland but also within a major conurbation. Words not on the hoardings are *property* and *bubble*.

The graft and innovation of the people who wore the stone from those steps played an important role in changing our culture.

Since then the productive forces of our species have grown exponentially. Cheap energy and robots are creating wealth which would have been unimaginable when the abbey was built. Yet people are working longer hours often in return for diminishing pay, and many can't afford secure housing.

The prolongation of the working-day beyond the limits of the natural day, into the night, only acts as a palliative. It quenches only in a slight degree the vampire thirst for the living blood of labour. To appropriate labour during all the 24 hours of the day is, therefore, the inherent tendency of capitalist production. KARL MARX

I wonder what the ancestors would think of it all, and I wonder what future generations will think when they look back on us as their ancestors.

***

The motorbike is fixed and the time has come to say bye to Mum. It's heartbreaking because, owing to her advanced years, neither of us know if we'll see each other again. But at least she likes to hear about my harebrained schemes, and the latest one seems to please her. I'm going in search of another mermaid.

MERMAIDS

If your heart is broken, make art with the pieces.

SHANE KOYCZAN

My recent interest in mermaids has been sparked by that short fling with a swimmer. She moved so gracefully in the water I came to suspect she terminated in a fish's tail. Though we swam and frolicked and had fun together I should have expected the inevitable – that she would swim away, leaving a sad sailor in her wake.

On this adventure I'm going in search of a different mermaid. This one lives in the shadow of Kinder Scout, the highest point in the landlocked Derbyshire Peak District. For once the toponymy is accurate – her home is called Mermaid's Pool. I'm wondering if she's lonely some five hundred metres above sea level in that barren, inhospitable landscape. But maybe not, as it is said her lake is connected to the Atlantic by underground caves. Folklore has it that if you swim there your health will improve, and if you swim there at midsummer she will grant you eternal life.

This is not the sort of place you'd expect the class antagonisms of British society to be played out, but in 1932 Britain was a political cauldron, and on 24 April that year five hundred working-class folk from the nearby industrial centres of Sheffield and Manchester, organised by 21-year-old communist Benny Rothmans, were about to make history on that very hillside.

The trespassers were politically aware workers, their purpose to demand the right to roam on the open land where, after the daily grind of manual labour, they liked to walk. When they did so they were often subjected to violence and intimidation from the Duke's employees. On that day they met in two groups, the Sheffield contingent to the east, the Manchester to the west. The landowner the Duke of Devonshire's gamekeepers were armed with sticks, and had their instructions: 'keep the rabble off the duke's land.' Police were on hand, as were sycophantic council officials. Photos of the day show the trespassers, many in shorts with spectacularly muscular legs, legs which out-walked their adversaries. The communists out-smarted police and gamekeepers, enabling the workers to reach their objective: to congregate on Kinder Scout.

Trespass is not a criminal offence, yet there were six arrests. I have my own experience of concocted evidence and can therefore imagine the likely scenario on Kinder that day: the witness statements very likely a work of creative fiction, a collaboration between the duke's men and the police. The Duke didn't need this land. Like many of his peers, past and present, he used it only occasionally for the shooting of small feathered creatures, after which the Duke and his associates would retire to the Manor House for aperitifs, vol-au-vents and a dinner of grouse served on a silver platter. Shooting grouse remains an elite pastime. Gunning them down will cost you as much as £7,000 per person per day. Gamekeepers from the grouse estates kill endangered birds of prey in order to protect their money-making targets. Huge tracts of open land are put by for this activity, which is subsidised by the UK taxpayer to the tune of £56 per year per hectare, indicating that the Kinder trespassers' work is still incomplete.

***

At the time of the trespass my Mum's dad, Tom, would have been twenty-nine years old. So far as I know he wasn't there that day, but he was a card-carrying socialist and just the sort of guy to get involved. His dad died when he was thirteen, whereupon, as eldest son, he was sent to work in the local coal mine as the family's sole breadwinner. A tough, stocky Yorkshireman, he claimed he'd hardly grown since being 'sent down pit' – which is plausible, because not only was the work physically demanding, in the winter months miners would have started and finished work in the dark, and so would likely have been vitamin D deficient.

The Kinder Trespass was part of a wider struggle for social justice and a better society, one in which children like my grandad wouldn't have to work in coal mines. On a nostalgic visit to Tom's home town of South Elmsall, I walked around the settlement's graveyard, and as testament to the things he told me, I founnd many headstones bearing the inscription, *So and So . . . killed in an accident at Frickley Colliery.*

Unlike me, Grandpa was teetotal. He taught himself Esperanto, a made-up, easy-to-learn language based on Spanish, which was born out of a spirit of internationalism and takes its name from the word *esperar*, hope in Spanish. The hope was that the language could stop war by bringing about a working class unified across nations. Obviously it didn't work, but such was the political climate in which the Kinder mass trespass took place. Some of the trespassers would be killed a few years later fighting as volunteers against fascism in the Spanish Civil War. And no doubt many more would be killed fighting it during the Second World War.

All those arrested on Kinder received prison sentences, but the publicity generated by their trials gave an important boost to the campaign for the right to roam, and laid the foundations for the creation of the National Parks, the first of which is centred on Kinder Scout itself. What a show was put on for the mermaid that day. Or perhaps it was she who used her special powers to help the trespassers.

***

En route from Leeds to London I visit Lauren, an old friend who lives in Sheffield. She's keen to come on the Mermaid Adventure. She's an artist and is the only person I know to have made her own coffin. She was using it as a wardrobe until 'D Day'. But thankfully she has outlived the wooden sarcophagus, which got woodworm and had to be unceremoniously dumped.

The morning of the Mermaid's Pool swim the forecast is for rain all day. After a miserable motorbike ride from Sheffield during which my waterproof trousers fail to meet their key performance indicator, we park up in the small settlement of Hayfield and set off on foot across country for the final few miles. This mostly treeless landscape is all about water, and today gravity is pulling it from the sky and dragging it down hillsides into gurgling streams and rivers, on to its temporary resting place in Kinder Reservoir.

Around halfway the footpath disappears and the going becomes slow on the steep, bracken-covered hillside. The absence of a footpath indicates that the Mermaid's home isn't well visited. Double checking our position using a map and compass, I'm confused. The pool should have been east of us. The compass says west. What mistake have I made? It takes a while to figure out that the compass is out by 180 degrees. I've been keeping it in a bag which attaches to the motorbike petrol tank with magnets. The magnets have reversed its polarity. In some situations that could be a terminal error.

A direct route would mean too many descents and climbs across the crenulated landscape, so we traverse the hillside at a constant height following what would be contour lines on a map. I fall as my foot disappears down a hole concealed by heather. Through it I can see and hear an underground stream.

After walking for an hour and a half we climb a stone wall and crest a ridge, and there it is, fifty metres away and a few metres below, on a small plateau of sheep-grazed grass. The brown, silent, mysterious water of Mermaid's Pool, bleak and inhospitable.

The natural world often mimics human culture, and the water in this landscape makes me think about the economic theory of *trickle down*. But a couple of miles away I can see water cascading over the dark brown rocky edge of Kinder Downfall, which is, in theory, a waterfall, except the wind today is strong enough to defy gravity, reversing the torrent, sending it back upwards as spray. Not so much downfall as upblow, nature's demonstration of how money moves around a free market economy in the real world.

Though the rain keeps falling, we're warm after the climb so we decide to get straight in, but not before making an offering to the lady of the lake. We don't want an angry mermaid situation, so we think it best to show our visit is well intentioned. Lauren makes a short speech. *We come in peace and wish you well and if you'd like to come back with us on the motorbike that would be fine.*

A mermaid on a motorcycle, that would not be average. We leave her some flapjack on a nearby rock and strip off. The lake is shallow and muddy at the sides. The water is cold. Lauren stays in for about five seconds. I'm happy to be on my own with the mermaid. Will she show herself? Through my goggles the peaty water makes my hand look orange. I stop swimming, lie on my back and let the water support me. I wait, turn on my front and have a good look around. I guess she must be in the Atlantic today, but somehow I know she knows we're there, and that she's happy about our presence.

After the swim Lauren and I sit beside the pool, drink our flasks of tea and relish our packed lunch in the rain, while enjoying the open vistas. There is something about big uninhabited terrain which always makes wonder how the ancestors lived in it.

It rains all the way back to Sheffield. I vow to get a new pair of waterproof trousers.

***

Have confidence that if you have done a little thing well, you can do a bigger thing well too.

DAVID STOREY

Gradually I'm gaining confidence, swimming in bigger waves and farther from land, slowly feeling less fearful. And what's happening in the sea is carrying over into life on land. Being a romantic I'm thinking maybe the Mermaid of Kinder has something to do with it.

Nicky (of the Peacehaven swim) and I have a plan which will test this newfound confidence – though it's already being challenged by an opposing feeling of apprehension as we walk down to the beach. We arrive at the lifeguard station, tell them our plan and leave our bags. Am I imagining it, or do the lifeguards look concerned?

Both of us have tow-floats, inflatable high-visibility sausages designed to make a swimmer easy to spot in the water. Ours also have a cargo-carrying capacity, in this case towel, clothes, shoes and a packed lunch. This will be my longest ever sea swim, from Brighton's West Pier to Hove Lagoon. Nicky suggests I wear the wetsuit. I decide not to.

Because your eyes are only a few centimetres above the sea surface, even relatively small waves make it difficult to see other swimmers. It is therefore likely Nicky and I will become separated during this adventure.

We swim out and turn west parallel with the shore, heading diagonally into the metre-high waves which slow us and make keeping a straight course difficult. Occasionally I can feel the tow-float pulling but the resistance is minimal.

Two hundred metres from shore and civilisation feels distant. I soon lose sight of Nicky – out here in these waves a person could drown unnoticed. In this place I'm truly captain of my own soul. Despite, or perhaps because of, being out of my comfort zone, I feel a sense of freedom. This is the opposite of a prison cell.

Occasionally I stop and look for Nicky but can't see her. The buildings on the coast road look tiny from out here. I can see the current is taking me slowly west. Stopping again, looking at the distant beach, I can see another lifeguard station with its yellow and red flags. I think I can see one of the lifeguards standing up and looking through binoculars but I'm not sure. Everything is in motion, the waves are relentless. I find maintaining mental calm in this chaotic sea requires effort.

Ahead I see Nicky and her orange tow-float. Each of us checks the other is OK and we swim on. Soon I'm alone again. Occasionally a young herring gull hovers a couple of metres above. I wonder why it's interested in me. Am I potential food? One of my eyeballs might make a tasty morsel. Or maybe it's just curious. One swimmer reported being pecked on the head by a gull. Whatever, I'm happy my eyes are behind goggles, leaving me free to enjoy being on the margins of their world.

After fifty minutes I feel cold but I'm not going to give up easily. I look towards land; the current has stopped flowing westward, which means it will soon turn against us. I can't recognise any landmarks, possibly because I'm cold and can't think straight. I put my head down, and swim on.

Back on land I may be a useless idiot, the sort of loser who misses diary appointments, drinks too much and can't hold down a proper job. All that's totally irrelevant out here. In the sea I'm just a person swimming and trying to stay alive. I stop again but still can't place myself. Ten minutes later I recognise the buildings on land and figure there's only another ten minutes to go. After an hour and twenty minutes I can see Nicky on the beach. I swim in and try to stand, and immediately fall over. Nicky helps me back to my feet.

We extract flasks and sandwiches from our tow-floats and feel a happy sense of achievement while picnicking on a bench on the prom. We walk back to our starting point. The lifeguards are curious; 'Did you make it?' they ask. Pointless though the swim may have been, we both feel a sense of achievement in saying, 'yes we did'. I wonder if it isn't the pointless things in life that are the most important?

***

Where does a thought go when it's forgotten?

SIGMUND FREUD

You know those sleepless nights when you're tossing and turning, contemplating life, with feelings of failure going round and round? I was thinking about something a friend had asked me that evening – 'have I been sabotaging myself?' It wasn't a shock revelation. I started at the top and worked my way down. Not exactly true, but Groucho Marx jokes always work for me, and it is true, I have thrown away many opportunities.

So there I am in bed thinking about self-sabotage. It's the middle of the night and perspective is lost, or perhaps in its loss it's been gained. In my mind's eye I see a shadowy figure. I can feel his presence. He's dressed all in black and carrying something. It's a limpet mine on a timer. He dives under water ready to attach his bomb. He's diving into my subconscious, but then he realises I've rumbled him. He panics and swims for shore, reaches land and runs off into the darkness taking his bomb with him. I know he'll be back. Then I start shaking and have the realisation that this psychic hijacker has been hiding in some corner of my being forever. Then I fall asleep. Or was I already asleep?

I wake in the morning wondering what to make of this strange experience. It was so real and it's convinced me that I do indeed have the psychological equivalent of an intestinal worm aboard. Googling psychic worming tablets produces no useful results.

HARE

You should not restrict yourselves to learning to see water from the viewpoint of human beings alone. Know that you must see water in the way that water sees water.

ZEN MASTER DOGEN

Donaudampfschifffahrtskapitänsmütze is the longest word in the German language. It means 'Danube steamship company captain's hat'. What would the German word be for *my uncle's captain's hat sat on my uncle's coffin*? Would this be a longer word in German?

Though sad, these are some of the thoughts going through my unruly ADHD mind as I watch Uncle Roger's coffin (with his captain's hat on its lid) being carried through a tunnel of oars held aloft by the crew of the lifeboat station he helped set up.

After Uncle Roger's funeral in Southampton I travel to my dad's place in Devon. The next morning it's still dark outside when the alarm goes off. I stuffed my face last night and will have a hearty breakfast this morning because I'm going to be burning a lot of energy. I throw my swimming things into a backpack, including the wetsuit, which hasn't seen the light of day for months. I leave the house at six.

As I walk through the sleepy Devon hamlet, the sky to the east is glowing in shades of purple tinged with yellow. The boats moored down on the river show themselves as dots set on a backdrop of glossy dark blue. I turn inland and walk up a steep country lane to a farmyard, where I meet a handful of other people also carrying backpacks. A small rickety bus arrives and carries us to the town of Totnes, a magnet for people who wear baggy patchwork trousers and believe in the power of crystals.

We disembark next to a rowing club on the banks of the River Dart. A sense of anticipation hangs in the air amongst the eight hundred or so people who are about to swim ten kilometres along the Dart from Totnes to Dittisham. It's an organised swim called the Dart 10k.

I've long been uneasy about swimming in rivers, but my hesitancy has been overwhelmed by a keenness to take part in this well-known event. But my reservations mean I've been monitoring the weather forecast, and when it predicts heavy rain for the second day of the event, I ask the organisers to move my entry to the first, because I know the sewage works in Totnes is likely to overflow into the river. (My concern is proved correct, because many of the Sunday swimmers become sick.)

Shoulder to shoulder, swimmers walk down a slipway and launch themselves into the river. Through goggles the water is murky and full of bubbles churned up by flailing limbs. There are hundreds of heads wearing brightly coloured swim hats. Minor collisions are frequent. I break for the outer edge of the pack. Though I can easily swim for a couple of hours without a wetsuit, the resistance offered by the neoprene means I have to use muscles which aren't required when swimming au naturel. Wearing the suit I feel disconnected from the water, but at no point do I feel even slightly cold. Soon I find a rhythm and up the pace.

Between start and finish there are two floating feeding stations at which the scene is reminiscent of some waterborne humanitarian disaster. On the menu are rapidly metabolised carbohydrates, fizzy drinks, jelly babies and bananas. I down a bottle of sugary pop while treading water and throw the empty back on the pontoon.

Much of the time I'm in a trance-like state where time stands still. But on occasions thinking occurs, and I find myself wondering what intelligent life forms such as dolphins would make of this procession of slow-moving land-dwelling mammals dressed in rubber. I ponder what Zen Master Dogen had in mind when he advised us to see water as water sees itself. Is this from the Zen school of *what is the sound of one hand clapping?* As my body passes through the murky river I muse on how it experiences me, how my body pushes water away from itself leaving a hole in it, an imprint of me. It's a moving anti-sculpture of myself.

The vortices, wavelets and bubbles I leave in my wake will quickly die, but according to chaos theory they matter. I have left an irreversible mark on the universe which will reverberate for all time. I wonder if chaos theory and laws of Karma are one and the same.

My dad, a sailor of considerable experience, advised me to take the bends in the river as wide as possible, because we will be swimming with the current which is always strongest on the outside of a bend. I heed his advice, and at times this means I'm well away from the main body of swimmers. Before the race started there was talk of waves. But after swimming in the English Channel I have little concern for the small waves on the Dart.

My head swings round with my body left and right every three strokes to take in air. This gives only an intermittent view of land; mostly one eye remains below the surface even when my head is rotated. Swimming isn't the best way to observe the surroundings, so occasionally I lift my head to see where I'm going and take in the dense oak woodland on the riverbank. The shoreline is craggy with granite rock. There are few habitations or signs of human intervention. My lonely current-seeking track takes me close to a solitary boathouse. There's a man sitting in the open downstairs window. I feel the urge to make a connection with him and say hello. He gives me a hello back. I feel extremely happy about this beautiful experience.

I start swimming faster, which means I need more air. So now I'm breathing on one side, every second stroke, to the right. Time has moved into another dimension and is passing unpredictably and I don't know what to expect when I remember to look at my watch. Periodically I float on my back just to savour the environment.

Swimmers are wearing one of five different coloured hats. Each entrant selected their own colour when signing up for the event:

Yellow – leisurely.
Red – medium.
White – fast.
Blue – elite.
Gold – for folks who have done three or more Dart 10k swims.

I'm in yellow. Within the main body of swimmers collisions are frequent, which makes me feel stressed. Soon I start feeling negative towards swimmers in caps of other colours. I start competing with some white caps who are trying to overtake. The feeling builds from negativity to hostility. Social science experiments have demonstrated how quickly humans organise themselves into groups hostile to outsiders, and I'm shocked to see how quickly I've succumbed.

I accidentally almost swim over a guy. I stop and look at him – a red cap. 'Serves him right,' I think, then I notice he looks terrified. The hostility evaporates and morphs into guilt. I say sorry and swim on. When I glance back he's still there, looking frightened and uncomfortable.

I've learned another small lesson about myself – I'm not immune to idiotic group-think. I make an effort to push the guilty feelings out of my mind because I selfishly want to enjoy this experience. I finish the swim at a sprint. I walk out of the water feeling tired in a happy way. My confidence as a human being has been given another small boost.

***

The man who is swimming against the stream knows the strength of it.

WOODROW WILSON

Preparing to leave Dittisham, packing the motorcycle panniers, I roll up the black tie I wore for Uncle Roger's send-off and wonder whose funeral I'll be wearing it at next – and as usual before a long journey on the motorbike, I wonder if it might be my own.

Just after dawn, with Devon still asleep, I twist the throttle, and the old motorbike and its hydrocarbon fuel pulls me up the hill out of the village. There's a large rabbit in the middle of this quiet country lane. It sees me and hops off, travelling in the same direction. I realise I've misidentified the animal; it's a hare. The beautiful big-eared creature lopes off into a field and is gone, leaving me smiling under my crash helmet.

Heading east back home I ride in low cloud for the first hour. Tiny water drops build up on the visor, which I wipe frequently with the back of my gloves. Then the sun comes out, drying my waxed cotton jacket.

After a couple of hours I need a break and notice some unusual-looking roof details in a town over to the left. I turn off the main road and ride into the settlement. The architecture could be Scandinavian. There are no road markings or signposts. The buildings look new, their design isn't familiar. I'm reminded of my first job as a hod carrier – a bricklayer's labourer. The roads serving the housing estates we were building hadn't been given the finishing touches of road markings or signposts. These new neighbourhoods were a blank canvas waiting for their history to arrive. This strange town has the same feeling. Ground zero for the future.

In the absence of road markings and signs, I ride slowly and cautiously. The buildings are all finished. There are shops and people. This isn't a town under construction. I ride around trying to figure the place out. There are few cars and lots of parking spaces. I pull up outside a café where I order coffee and a sandwich. Am I imagining it, or are people unfriendly? I sit at a table outside in the sun.

The café owner, a middle-aged, conservatively dressed white woman, brings my coffee. I'm friendly towards her and ask why there aren't any road markings. Her face doesn't crack. 'We don't have them in this town,' she says and leaves. I speculate on the possibility of her being a robot. Maybe I've passed into a parallel dimension. It's unnerving. I look at my watch, half expecting to see it's stopped. The second hand is still moving.

I could've unknowingly strayed onto a movie set. These people are all actors improvising in a Mike Leigh film and they think I'm playing the bad guy. The cafébot returns with my sandwich. I pretend she's not being hostile and try again. She reluctantly tells me the place was designed without signposts or road markings. She doesn't tell me why.

A daring couple sit at a table near me. I'm feeling paranoid. I remind myself that just because I'm paranoid doesn't mean they're not out to get me. I talk to the couple. Throughout the whole interaction the guy never says a word and his face remains expressionless. He too could be a droid. The woman reluctantly tells me the place is called Poundbury, and that it was recently built by the Duchy of Cornwall as an extension to the nearby town of Dorchester.

She tells me the Duchy of Cornwall means Prince Charles. He apparently doesn't like signs. I'm surprised to find that HRH and I have something in common. He apparently doesn't like road markings either. He's right, pointless signs are everywhere, which means no one reads them – even that really useful one which says *minefield.*

***

According to Wikipedia . . .

Poundbury is a high density urban quarter of Dorchester. It gives priority to people, rather than cars, and commercial buildings are mixed with residential areas, shops and leisure facilities to create a walkable community. The result is an attractive and pleasing place, in keeping with the character of Dorchester, in which people live, work, shop and play.

The idea of Shared Space for pedestrians and vehicles started in Holland. In this model of traffic management there are no pavements, the whole street is on one level without road markings or kerbs. Counterintuitively this changes the behaviour of drivers who respond by reducing their speed and upping their caution, just as I instinctively did when I drove into the town.

The theory is that a delineation between pavement and road, usually provided by a kerb, and a system of priority at junctions, all declared by signs, permits drivers to abdicate responsibility. All they have to do is follow rules. You could say the Shared Space system is a form of anarchy in which the rules of hierarchical authority are dumped in favour of an overriding and universally understood imperative – not to hurt another human being.

Poundbury leaves me feeling confused. I like the traffic management system, but the place feels contrived, like a theme park version of an English town. And I, correctly identified as different, attract mindless micro-hostility. I get the feeling HRH was trying to do good with his Poundbury project, but the place had more than a whiff of paternalism and reminded me of Saltaire, a Yorkshire town built in the 1800s by mill owner Titus Salt for his workers. He sensibly banned alcohol and not very modestly named the place after himself. But today, with Salt long dead, the last laugh goes to an off-licence in the village called Don't Tell Titus.

I resist the urge to graffiti 'Up the Republic' on the town walls, and my joke about Poundland headquartering itself in the place goes down like a lead balloon with the café owner. Poundbury makes me feel about as welcome as a faecal accident in a swimming pool, and I feel a sense of relief riding out of town.

GNASHERS

Everything you can imagine is real.

PABLO PICASSO

In the British Isles the combination of light winds, warm air, warm sea, small waves and moonlight is rare. This evening is one of those occasions. Forward planning amounts to obtaining a small waterproof red light, which in theory will make me visible in the water.

I walk down the hill to the beach in shorts and flip-flops, feeling the velvety summer air on my skin. The moon is a few days after full and hangs in a cloudless sky, giving enough light to make out huddles of people socialising on the beach. Opposite the bandstand east of a hefty stone-built breakwater, I see an angler wearing a head torch. He's fiddling with his rods and looks like he'll be there for some time, so I ask if he'll keep an eye on my bag. 'No problem, leave it by my chair,' he says.

I sit on the shingle looking seaward. Ten miles offshore are the lights on barges being used for the construction of the Rampion Windfarm. Seventy-five miles beyond them is France. I see a red flash five hundred metres out to sea; it's the light mounted on West Pier Buoy, the purpose of which is to warn mariners of the hazard to navigation that are the remains of the pier after it was destroyed by three arson attacks in two months back in 2003. In the moonlight I can just make out its rusting steel skeleton. My plan is to swim around the buoy and back. This will be my first night swim. It'll be about a kilometre over the seabed, further through the water owing to the current. I'm surprised by my lack of apprehension.

A few months after the pier fires in August 2003, West Pier Buoy mysteriously came loose and was discovered drifting off Shoreham Harbour. The navigation mark is anchored by a heavy chain attached to a substantial weight. To set it free would require equipment and effort. I rack my brains for a motive . . .

***

In 2003, as now, Brighton was awash with drugs, and smuggling them was paying top dollar. That same year, Colombian drug cartel boss Pablo Escobar had been non-compliant with the CIA and was therefore dead. His shoes had been filled by another Colombian, El Loco, whose confidence and power had escalated since his rival's death. El Loco's people had been experimenting with submarines for the purpose of smuggling narcotics. Little known is that he had also commissioned magnetic waterproof containers which could be attached below a navigation buoy's waterline, allowing small vessels to use them as drop-off and pick-up points for cash and contraband.

The first time the device was used in England was in 2003, when an operation to attach it to West Pier Buoy went wrong. The inexperienced crew of the courier vessel messed up and the magnetic box's safety cable got tangled with the buoy's mooring chain. With dawn coming they were forced to leave the container submerged, hanging in the depths. Two days later, three Colombians flew into London. Having hired divers and a local fishing boat from Newhaven, they cut West Pier Buoy free and recovered the magnetic box, containing two hundred kilograms of mind-altering chemicals.

The cartel gangsters had a sinister edge. The local fishermen might be tough but they'd never met anything like the Colombians; their lack of facial expression was unnerving. But the fishing had been poor that season, and the vessel's skeleton crew were happy with a year's pay for one night's work. The Colombian in charge said in a strong Spanish accent, 'You tell no one.' In a movie his character would have drawn a finger across his throat. But this was real life and the guy was scary enough without having to resort to theatrics. The crew and captain looked nervously at each other. They didn't even tell their wives. And so on Britain's south coast, during August and September 2003 there was no interruption to the supply of cocaine. The self-medicators, whether battling depression, fighting feelings of futility and inadequacy or just seeking fun, continued spending their money getting high.

***

As it's dark I think about making the swim naked, but for the sake of the nearby fishermen I decide not to. Also, it hasn't happened yet, but there's the possibility of going in starkers then finding things go wrong, meaning you have to land in a place your clothes aren't. I fix the light to my goggles strap and switch it to flashing.

A gentle swell is rattling the shingle. The sea is almost flat. I wade in, put my head down and feel the water against my skin. I swim out at right angles to the beach and smile when I see my hands are stirring up the sea's version of shooting stars, trails of green bioluminescence. A couple of hundred metres out I stop to get my bearings. The dark silhouette of tangled steel, all that remains of the pier, is just visible, but I can't see the buoy. Then its light flashes one short red, and once I've located it I can also make out its dark dome shape against the night horizon.

The moon leaves its reflection on the sea. My track will be a little left of its silvery invitation to infinity. I think about sea creatures and their teeth. I think about drunks in a speedboat running me down, but the nearest drunks are onshore half a kilometre away, and what about the risk of staying on land and doing nothing? I think about El Loco's men, but that was just a story – or was it? I feel calm and swim on.

I am surprised to see the buoy isn't getting closer and I'm further from shore than intended. From this I can tell the current is running west faster than I expected. I must now swim directly east parallel to the beach. I up my pace and because of this I need more air, so I'm breathing mostly to my right every other stroke. I stop briefly every few minutes to check the distance. Giving up crosses my mind, but my whole life I've been swimming against the current one way or another and giving up isn't something I'm about to do easily. Then I see the distance is slowly closing. I feel strong but at the same time I'm aware of my insignificance. Every second ten million tonnes of water are dragged by the moon and sun's gravity west down the English Channel. I'm immersed in planetary forces incalculably stronger than myself.

I reach the buoy. It's much bigger than it looks from land, maybe three metres tall. I don't want to make contact with its barnacled underside, and as the current could pull me back onto it, I give it a wide berth. After rounding it I head directly for shore in the knowledge the current will take me back westwards. The buildings on shore look small. I feel disconnected from land. There are unlit metal buoys in the water and swimming headfirst into one would hurt, so I stop frequently, struggling to make them out against the bright lights of the seafront.

It's not far to humanity, but it might as well be a million miles. This is a silent, lonely, unpopulated place, where the imagination is free. I wonder what it would be like to see all the lights on land go out, for humankind to come to an end. I make landfall to find everyone gone. Just me and the mermaids left on this ball floating in space. I feel strangely comfortable with the idea. I almost look forward to it being true.

Around forty minutes after leaving the beach, I return to land. The lights are still on and humanity hasn't come to an end. I say hi to the fisherman, who is still fiddling with his rods. He tells me he's caught a big bass. I wonder if my safety light makes me visible in the water, so I ask him if he saw where I swam. 'Oh yes,' he says, 'you went that way,' and points west in the opposite direction.

***

Try to understand the blackness, lethargy, hopelessness, and loneliness they're going through. Be there for them when they come through the other side. It's hard to be a friend to someone who's depressed, but it is one of the kindest, noblest, and best things you will ever do.

STEPHEN FRY

Back home in London, the hound has returned. I feel like a basket case. It's as though my head is collapsing in on itself, pulling my forehead into the centre of my brain. I can't think clearly and feel powerless. Somehow I manage to get myself to the lido. As soon as I'm walking down the side of the pool I feel the brain crushing begin to lift and immediately I start swimming the black dog disappears. Looks like I can out-swim the bastard.

***

Chaos is inherent in all compounded things. Strive on with diligence.

BUDDHA

'This toothpaste tastes strange,' I think to myself. The next time

I brush with the herb-tasting dental cleanser my friend has left on the boat, I absent-mindedly read the label, and discover it's actually Factor 50 suncream. I smile in the knowledge that I'm in no danger of getting sunburned gnashers, while inside the error triggers my anxiety about the difficulties I have in organising myself. A similar pattern of emotions crowd my mind when I discover that I've been wearing my swimming trunks back to front for at least a year. My inability to organise is a flaw which has adversely affected every area of my life.

The cherry on the cake of my disorganisation came the day after the night I'd spent tossing and turning thinking about the surgeon burrowing into my belly. For the last couple of months I'd been 'organising' my life around the date of the hernia operation. But on the day I discover I have put the wrong time in my diary. I'm too late and they can't do the operation. It's not dignified for a grown man to cry in public. I only just maintain a manly resilience.

Through my eyes a page of text or a list looks as though the script is jumbled, moving about on the page. When I finish a line of text and attempt to move my eyes to the next line I often return to the wrong place. This makes reading frustratingly slow. With shopping lists I'm strangely blind to some of the items and will usually miss at least one. A to-do list turns into a concept about as complicated as a tangle of knotted fishing line. As soon as I think about organising the future I feel anxious, largely due to the number of appointments I've missed. I'm pretty sure all this stems from years of minute-by-minute conditioning through humiliation at school. The upshot is a feedback loop of performance-inhibiting anxiety about the future. But I don't give up. I keep limping on.

We live in complicated times, and many people including myself work freelance, which requires organisational skills. Consequently the routes to organisational fuck-ups are multiplying.

This post-modern, post-industrial society also appears post-*understandable*.

If you are on a sinking ship or learning to swim you're likely to have a lifejacket or inflatable armbands. I acknowledge computers have advantages – I couldn't write without spellcheck and a computer. But unless you count antidepressants, no such device exists to help you swim in the waters of the digital era.

Having missed the operation, to cope with my feelings of despair, I take myself to the lido for a two-hour swim. Afterwards I return to the changing room and discover someone has stolen my new sneakers.

I cycle home in a pair of flip-flops given to me by the lifeguards, change into some shoes and go to a nearby shop to buy groceries. On the way there I come across a man lying on the ground next to a smashed motorbike. I stop to help. I think he may have a broken pelvis. He asks for something to be put under his head. I use my rucksack. His *friend* is nearby in an agitated state; his shouting is distressing the man on the ground. When I try to explain this to Mr Shouty, he threatens to kill me. I take his threat seriously, but my bag is under the injured man's head. A crowd has gathered. I ask someone else to put something under the guy's head and escape with my herniated life.

That evening I drink more than usual.

RECIDIVISTS

Money often costs too much.

RALPH WALDO EMERSON

Because of the high cost of office space, the Port of London Authority is humiliated by being unable to afford a central London HQ overlooking the river it manages. Instead they slum it a block north in a little backstreet opposite St Dunstan-in-the-East, a ruined church dating from 1100. I'm here to ask permission to swim across the Thames.

The contrasting architecture of the old church and its neighbouring buildings impart a feeling of lineage, which offsets the unease I feel about being in the vortex of two evils, the Port of London Authority and capitalism.

St Dunstan's Church has suffered considerable misfortune – amputation, prosthetic, fire and explosions. It was badly damaged in the Great Fire of London but patched up, and between 1695 and 1701 it had a spire added which was designed by the renowned London architect Christopher Wren. The Luftwaffe commissioned its most significant alteration, after which it was never completely repaired. Its grounds are now a peaceful respite from the hurly-burly of the City.

Whenever I enter the Square Mile I feel uncomfortable. You can smell the money, and let's face it, the City's coat of arms isn't a smiley face; it's a sinister, spiky-looking dragon and bears the words DOMINA DIRIGE NOS, meaning *Lord Guide Us* in Latin.

One can only assume the Lord wasn't listening, or the advice administered by the Lord was ignored, because the place is consecrated to God's nemesis – Mammon. The City has previous for extortion, armed robbery and kidnap (aka the slave trade and colonialism). They'd have you believe they aren't recidivists. I'm not convinced.

I enter the PLA's office building. It's unremarkable, just one more swanky property development. A black concierge with an African accent shows me into a lift. On the first floor I find white men sitting at computers, all wearing shirts that match their complexion. I realise these are virtual harbourmasters; like most office workers, they look like they need more sun, but unlike other office workers they have gold on their epaulettes, which reminds me of Uncle Roger. One of them sports a huge beard and looks like Captain Haddock.

A clean-shaven junior harbourmaster shows me into a glitzy conference room with a huge oval table, across which we chat about motorcycles, boats and the Thames. He's a former Thames skipper and is knowledgeable about the river. I'm only slightly surprised he hasn't heard of the *Princess Alice* disaster; few people have. Could that be because unlike the *Titanic*, no aristocrats perished, its casualties all working-class Londoners?

I give him details of the proposed swim. He gives me the corporate spiel: 'The PLA want to facilitate use of the river.' I don't believe him.

***

Just because nobody complains doesn't mean all parachutes are perfect.

BENNY HILL

I walk into the room and am directed to sit on a black padded platform. The space is like some secret windowless bunker, a magical domain, the quality of the light and the quiet are the prequel to something. The energy is that of a temple. Powerful feng shui is focused on one central location; it could be the altar of some long-forgotten belief system fused with the futuristic equipment of science fiction. I'm at the centre, I'm on the altar, at the focal point, and the ritual is about to commence. I'm feeling nervous. I'm at the heart of an institution. An inner voice is screaming at me to get out, to run, not only out of the room but out of the building.

'Where would you like to go on holiday?' asks a man who has just pumped a few cubic centimetres of liquid into me. I imagine swimming in the blue waters of Greece, then I wake up on a trolley moving through a hospital corridor. People are looking at me. I want to tell them not to, but I have no voice and no strength.

After my organisational fiasco the hernia op was rescheduled and so here I am in a fluffy drug-induced world. I feel relaxed. Only a bit less so when the high priest of medicine appears through the curtains. The surgeon looks tense as he tells me he found and repaired seven hernias, not, as expected, two. I mustn't lift anything more than a carrier bag of shopping for two months. 'What about swimming?' I ask. 'Not for a month, and not at full strength for two months.' Now I feel fearful. I thought I'd be back in the water after a week. It's going to be a balancing act between physical and mental survival. They want to keep me in hospital overnight. I want to resist, but I'm trying to be sensible, trying to comply with the institution.

The ward feels cosy. Everything feels cosy. These are nice drugs. I chat to the other inmates. The guy opposite has just had a cancer operation. He's self-administering morphine by pressing a button. In a quiet voice, through an almost toothless mouth set in a sad pale thin face, he tells me he has a five per cent chance of survival. I tell him I'll say a prayer for him; he seems to appreciate that. I don't know who I'm praying to, but I take a few moments all the same.

Next to him is a chatty guy, a retired bus driver. And next to him an East End tough guy. A middle-aged black man is in the bed by the window. He's telling the nurse about being beaten up by the cops. In the bed next to mine is a retired white black-cab driver. Everyone except me is proper East London.

I love these guys and their stories. We're all in the shit together. The bus driver tells us about the time his brakes failed while driving a Routemaster, one of the old open-backed double-deckers. He aimed the machine for a big pile of sand, part of some roadworks. He had no way of knowing there was a skip full of rocks behind the sand. The bus engine was knocked backwards and took the legs off the passengers in the front seat. I guess the accident must have left him traumatised, which is probably why he's telling the story. The ex-taxi driver has a hernia. He's eighty-eight and weighing the odds of having an operation or leaving be.

***

A week after the operation and I'm struggling to follow the surgeon's instructions not to swim. The penalty for non-compliance could be the further punishment of yet more inactivity. I'm going through a rollercoaster of despair and regret. Regret for having the operation as I don't know if I can mentally survive the inactivity. The crutch of physical activity has been kicked away, the thing I had relied on to keep the depression at bay isn't possible right now. Perhaps it would have been better to take my chances and not have the operation. I don't have a time horizon and can't process any idea of a future. My brain is numb. It feels as though my heart is going to jump out of my chest. I need to be out of breath and feel the air pumping in and out of my lungs.

Lucky I live on a boat not in a tower block, because I feel like throwing myself off one.

I inspect my groin and there is a bulge where there shouldn't be. Does that mean the operation hasn't worked? Am I going crazy? I must have some addiction to chemicals produced by exercise and am suffering withdrawal. I am jittery, anxious and paranoid, I feel sure the hospital has done some kind of permanent damage to me. The bulge in my groin has grown. This means another trip to the hospital. I chat on the phone with a friend who tells me the drugs I've been given during the operation are probably the biggest dose I have ever taken. I would expect a come-down after party drugs, maybe this is the same kind of thing.

Trying to distract myself, I go online. An email from the clean-shaven junior harbourmaster at the PLA informs me my proposed swim does not have their approval. Right now I couldn't care less.

I find it difficult to trust the System. Why did I let them into my body? When I see a knife in my kitchen I have a crazy urge to slice myself open and tear out the plastic sheet they left in me. I need to acknowledge that I am not thinking straight and that neither medicine nor the System are always bad and dangerous. My dad and his wife were both cured of cancer, and so was Harry, my nun-for-a-year friend.

After the operation I spoke to the surgeon's understudy, who was giving the NHS a plug, asking if I knew how much it would have cost to have seven hernias repaired privately. £20,000. I should be grateful.

A couple of nights later I'm back at the hospital, where a doctor squeezes and prods my bruised groin. He isn't sure why there is a bulge but he doesn't believe I've herniated again. He thinks it could be something to do with my sperm ducts. They will do a scan on me sometime in the future. He gives me an NHS jock-strap. Hey, I was feeling low and alone – now I have support.

Back home on the boat I distract myself by writing a few words for the Ghosts of Gallions Reach and ask myself if bad poetry is better than none . . .

Princess Alice.
A poisoned chalice

She's got no loyalty
You can't trust royalty

The Captains gambled.
Puppet strings tangled

Some say the Captain was a clown
The dice took you down

This ship was just for Christmas
So speaks the witnes

I have time on my hands so I Google *anatomy of the male reproductive system* because of my suspected sperm duct swelling. Some time later I Google *capitalism*, wondering if the word should begin with a capital letter. As far as some algorithm is concerned, I have an interest in men's privates and capitalism. It has linked the two interests and the search returns *the Intelligent homosexual's guide to capitalism*.

***

Because I have concerns about my mental health I have swum earlier than advised. It's been gentle and sedate, moving my torso as little as possible and only for an hour at a time.

The surgeon advised I could ride the motorbike after two weeks. I suspect the surgeon knows a lot less about riding motorbikes than he does about mending people. It's a heavy old machine, so I leave it three weeks before riding down to Brighton for a short swim in the sea. I figure the tightness of the wetsuit should prevent my guts becoming free-floating entities in the English Channel.

The swimming has helped. Consequently some level of mental equilibrium has returned.

MORTAL

Aspirations? What I aspire to is being able to live contentedly without depression.

MIKE WELLS

It's the solstice, the shortest day of the year. Thanks to the NHS and the surgeon's skill my guts are now held in place by the plastic sheet he installed inside me, so I can swim without the wetsuit. It's mid-tide. There are about fifteen people on the beach including a few Brighton hippies, who are quick to get naked. Surprisingly for Brighton, the nakedness elicits some disapproving tuts from the few passers-by who are brave enough to endure the filthy weather.

The sea temperature is 8 °C. Without the rubber insulation, the cold is immediate, joint aching, burning. Breath control is difficult but necessary as the waves are breaking over my head. Gradually the feeling of cold subsides. I stick close to my friends. We bob for a bit, swim east, then turn back westwards, but we are still moving slowly backwards over land because the current is flowing east faster than we can swim. I can feel the cold sapping my strength, and trying to swim faster has no effect because my cold muscles lack power. We give up and swim directly back to the beach, then run back to our starting point. An eight-minute swim and I feel changed physically and mentally. Drying myself there's no feeling of cold, just an all-over numbness. But about five minutes later, the shivering begins.

Before swimming I sometimes rate my mood out of ten (the

inner bureaucrat). After immersion there's a mood uplift in the order of two points. The uplift usually lasts until the following day. The act of swimming is one thing. The act of swimming in cold water is something more.

***

Emotional pain cannot kill you, but running from it can. Allow. Embrace. Let yourself feel. Let yourself heal.

VERONICA TUGALEVA

Since the hernia operation something has changed. Pre-operation I didn't exactly feel invincible, but now I have an increased sense of vulnerability. Riding the motorbike feels dangerous and unappealing. Getting drunk and talking and listening to bullshit seems pointless – I'm still doing it, but it no longer counteracts the void or provides meaningful companionship.

***

Sat on the beach in Brighton with Nicky staring out to sea I feel horribly gloomy. It's one of those beautiful cold clear sunny winter's days, yet my spirit is unimpressed. My mood hovers at a 3. I'm not good company. The sea temperature has dropped and I feel reluctant to get in. Nicky is being persuasive. I know I should give it a try, if only as an experiment to see what happens to my mood. I undress my miserable self, put my trunks on (the right way round), and gloomily plunge myself into the English Channel.

Pain. My feet and hands feel as though they're being squeezed in a vice. There is a strong urge to run out of the sea and never do this again. It takes a minute or so to control my breathing. Despite the ice-cream head I eventually get my face in and swim. After about two minutes I check my mood and find I still feel depressed, but I can't focus on the depression because I have other things to deal with – like survival. I forget about being miserable and swim. As I make it back to our starting point I can feel my limbs losing power. I'm aware that if Nicky got into trouble I would have no spare capacity to help, but anyhow it's more likely I'd be the one needing help.

Ten minutes later I realise the knotted feeling in the centre of my forehead has vanished and the self-pitying depressive state has disappeared. I'm at a 6.5. I was in the water for seven minutes. I feel fresh and invigorated. Those seven minutes have changed everything.

FOOT

In the long run we are all dead.

JOHN MAYNARD KEYNES

The toing and froing between London and Brighton continues. I find myself living between two cities. Tonight I'm back on the boat on the River Lea in London where it's a cold night, -2 °C. Through the glass in the stove door I watch gently flaming logs which fill the cabin with heat. I feel grateful I have a warm and a cosy home, thankful I'm not one of those gerbil wheel casualties who end up on the streets on a cold winter's night.

I've always had a fear of homelessness. It stems from an inability to fit in, which leaves a person vulnerable to unemployment and its consequences. Add into the mix a sprinkle of mental ill-health and there you are without anywhere to live.

The other day I met a man with a poem called Foot. (It was the poem not the man that was called Foot. The man's name was Mo.) Sat in a doorway, he wanted to recite his work to me. It was a beautiful homage to feet and went through all the things we take for granted about those appendages farthest from our eyes. They carry us to loved ones, support us against the relentless force of gravity. Kept captive in shoes, they deserve more appreciation.

The encounter made me think of the morning after my breakdown in Harry's flat. She'd asked me to take a load of her unwanted tat to a nearby charity shop. Carrying her old guitar and carrier bags, with a large rucksack on my back, I was wondering why people were looking at me strangely, giving me a wide berth. They looked frightened. Then I twigged. Dishevelled, unshaven, unhappy and carrying lots of baggage, I looked homeless. I was surprised how how offended I felt. I wanted to say don't judge me, I'm a person too.

***

A salt doll arrives at the sea after a long journey across land. She has never seen the ocean before and is curious. She asks the sea, 'Who are you?' The water replies, 'I am the ocean. Come in and find out.' The doll walks into the waves and just before dissolving she declares, 'Now I understand who I am.'

BUDDHIST FABLE

The doctor tells me a swelling and soreness under my nipple is mastitis, an infection common in women but rarely found in men. She reckons I probably picked it up at the lido. I've been prescribed antibiotics and advised to stop swimming for a week; not good for my mental health. Consequently I'm at a mood quotient of 2.5 and feel like a useless lump of offal, unable to go into the world and without the motivation required to thrive.

That feeling of a vertical furrow in the centre of my forehead which reaches deep inside my skull is back. Often, when in this mental state, in social situations, my face muscles feel as though they are pulling in opposite directions. I want to grimace and growl but I put on a brave face. The reality of my emotional state conflicts with my will to hide it. Those two forces fight a battle which I can feel in my face, like two ferrets in a bag.

My ability to reason is diminished. I feel confused about time and my place in it. It's as though there is only now. Perhaps this is why I have such anxiety over diaries and organising. Although Harry tells me that in the world of meditators, 'being in the now' is a highly prized, but inevitably elusive goal, it doesn't benefit me.

Like the sea, all this ebbs and flows. I'm not always in a state of mental despair; sometimes I feel confident. I may be a failure, but at least my sense of being isn't built on an imagined self, not precariously based on what I own or on some position in the hierarchy. But that also has consequences. I feel a cultural gap between myself and many of those around me. I have a disregard for what many admire, and admire what many appear to disrespect. I am clueless about celebrities and royalty. Displays of wealth designed to impress leave me underwhelmed.

The construct of the 'self-made man' is widely accepted, which demonstrates a distorted view of our relationship with each other, our planet and all the other life forms on it. No one is self made.

For the sake of my mental health I need to swim but I can't for a few days more owing to the mastitis. My friend Ed advises me this is a case of tough titties.

***

There are known knowns. There are things we know that we know. There are known unknowns. That is to say, there are things that we now know we don't know. But there are also unknown unknowns. There are things we do not know we don't know.

DONALD RUMSFELD

I'm visiting hospital for a post-operation check-up. After a few prods and pokes the surgeon looks pleased and signs me off as repaired. I heap praise and thanks upon him. Feeling relieved, I get on my bicycle. Riding from the hospital grounds I stand on the pedals, but my foot finds no resistance. The chain has come off. My foot powers down and I'm thrown off balance. I lose control, veer off the road and crash headfirst into a man walking in the opposite direction.

The impact on the side of my head is significant – perhaps it was his shoulder I hit first. He is spun round and knocked over. I land on the ground next to him. He doesn't get up. 'Are you OK?' I say. After a pause he stammers, '*My back.*' I'm terrified I've seriously injured him.

Eventually he gets up, though he's in pain. We are surrounded by confused doctors on their lunch break. There isn't anything for them to do. Graciously, he accepts my apologies, saying he 'understands it was an accident'. I ask if he wants my contact details. He doesn't. A tall black man of about my age, he seems more reasonable than I might have been in his shoes.

What I don't tell the guy I crashed into is that a week ago the chain came off the bike and I nearly fell off. At that point I said to myself, 'I must fix the chain tensioner.' But I left it till *later*.

I go home and fix the bike, and renew my expired third party cycle insurance.

***

When a man is tired of London, he is tired of life.

SAMUEL JOHNSON

London, this pressure cooker of humanity, has been my home for nineteen years, longer than anywhere else, but finally it's time to leave this dirty old town. I'm getting ready to move off the boat, and onto land in Brighton.

Preparing to move makes me take stock of things here in the capital. One of the things I love about this city is that despite the inhumanity of its size, the stress and difficulties many of its inhabitants face, people mostly treat each other with kindness and respect. Terms of endearment – mate, love, darling – which strangers use towards each other always make me smile and I use them whenever I can. But I need to be near the sea and to swim in it every day. It's not so much a case of being tired of life, as of being tired of a life of depression.

WRESTLING

A story should only be believed once it's been officially denied.
MIKE WELLS

I've always had a fear of finding someone in difficulty in the water and not being able to rescue them. Now I'm actually living on the coast and spending lots of time on the beach, it makes sense to learn how to do so. So I've signed up for a one-week beach lifeguard course. But there is a problem – a qualifying requirement to swim 400 metres in less than eight minutes.

Simply putting in more effort gives negative results, I swim only slightly faster and tire faster. The harder I try the slower I become over the distance. Though strength and stamina are helpful, swimming is more about technique than brawn. (It's not about the Braun either, for those who remove body hair hoping they will go ever so slightly faster.)

Rather than working with the water I'm still fighting it. I'm wrestling with an entity which is entirely neutral about my existence. I am brawling with it because I'm still fearful and unskilful with it.

The swim test is held in a pool belonging to Roedean, the nation's best private school for girls. On the edge of Brighton, the place shows what serious money can buy a child. Its grand buildings stand in many hectares of manicured lawns which slope at a pleasing angle south towards the coast road. Beyond them the land terminates suddenly with chalk cliffs which plunge downwards into the sea, and where some unhappy folks terminate themselves.

As I cycle into Roedean's grounds the sun is sparkling off the English Channel. To the west there are views beyond Worthing towards Selsey Bill; to the south, just visible under the cliffs is Brighton Marina; and to the east, set in rolling downland, the Blind Veterans' Rehabilitation Centre. The magnificent views from the institution's huge glass windows are one of life's sad ironies.

Even before getting in the pool I feel nervous; my heart is thumping like a bass drum. Swimmers are being batch processed in groups of four. '*Go!*' says the guy with the stopwatch and we push off on our sixteen-length game of waterborne ping-pong. Straight away I'm breathing too hard. I'm not on form, still aching from the bicycle crash. 'Relax, don't fight the water,' I say to myself, and 'roll'. Things really don't feel right. I'm tense and breathing heavily, indicating I'm burning way too much energy. 'Ten lengths,' shouts the man with the stopwatch, then 'Fourteen.' Two lengths to go. I give it everything on those final two lengths. I touch and look up. 'Seven minutes fifty-four seconds,' says the man with the stopwatch. In a couple of months I'll be able to begin the lifeguard course.

Cycling happily out of Roedean's grounds, I see a purposeful-looking ship standing off Brighton beach. She has a distinctive blue hull, cream superstructure and a large crane mounted on her foredeck. I recognise her from the last time I saw her off Blackpool Sands in Devon.

***

Patricia is a Trinity House ship whose honourable task is to maintain navigation aids around the British Isles. From her position I can see she's about to lift West Pier Buoy, the navigation mark I swam around at night last summer. I want to watch this. Will there be evidence of a drugs stash box?

I hurry home for binoculars. Arriving back on the beach, I see through them that half the buoy's superstructure is missing, probably due to an error by a drunken sailor whose boat most likely came off a lot worse.

They swing the crane out over the starboard side. I have a perfect view of *Patricia*'s crew lifting the buoy clear of the water and onto her front deck. When they lift the buoy's chain and its anchor the whole ship to lists to starboard. Not surprising as the anchor looks like a giant iron bath plug and must weigh many tonnes. I'm disappointed to see there is no sign of anything suspicious under the buoy or attached to its chain.

The *official* story for the buoy breaking loose is that a swivel link in its mooring chain randomly failed . . .

***

Fear is the main source of superstition, and one of the main sources of cruelty. To conquer fear is the beginning of wisdom.

BERTRAND RUSSELL

Today's swim had an undercurrent of the macabre with a rescue helicopter hovering half a mile east and a number of boats searching nearby. Early in the morning a man holding a beer can was seen entering the sea naked. He wasn't seen coming out again. We all knew we were sharing the sea with a corpse.

I wondered what it would be like to find a body in the water. I could have asked one of the boaters from our community in London. She was traumatised by finding body parts in the canal next to her boat. They belonged to the victim of a gruesome murder in east London. I figure swimming into a decomposed body would be a lot more unpleasant than a fresh one.

The search proved unsuccessful and was called off after a few hours. Later in the day the dead man washed up on Hove beach opposite the Peace Angel statue.

***

I tried drowning my sorrows but the bastards learned to swim.

FRIDA KAHLO

Brighton has been my new home for about three weeks. It's the end of the winter and the sea temperature has remained at 11 °C for some time. Probably because of the swimming, the last three weeks have been depression free. But things are not OK. I'm forced into acknowledging that my drinking is out of control. Two bottles of wine a night cannot be sustainable. And if I'm at a party it could be more.

A crunch moment came one morning when I'd finished trimming my beard. Not part of my normal grooming routine, I used a small hand mirror to check my handiwork from the side. Shock horror, folds of flabby skin and a double chin. This tangible evidence of drink-induced damage forces me to look at the other effects of alcohol. The depression, the chaotic lifestyle and a back catalogue of failed relationships (my fault). Reality has collided with delusions. Though I'm aware it's an inadequate response, I'm vowing not to drink for a month.

REPRESSION

Our current mental-hygiene philosophy stresses the idea that people ought to be happy, that unhappiness is a symptom of maladjustment. Such a value system might be responsible for the fact that the burden of unavoidable unhappiness is increased by unhappiness about being unhappy.

EDITH WEISSKOPF-JOLSON

Misfortune is everywhere, unavoidable. In our culture huge quantities of drugs and alcohol are consumed in a bid to block out this reality, but when reality is pushed down it will bubble up elsewhere. My relationship with drugs and alcohol is based on the repression of such horrors and on a futile attempt to suppress depression, but I can't figure out how this knowledge changes anything.

I love that cosy feeling of inebriation and the knowledge that anyone I'm drinking with feels the same. It offers comfort in a difficult and often hostile world. While alcohol circulates I become chattier, funnier and easier to be with – at least I think I do. But even if, in the short term, there is some social advantage, in my heart I know that in the long run alcohol extracts its toll, and my beverage balance sheet is showing a deficit.

Memo to self: reasons not to drink . . .

Flabby face and other bits
Reduction in energy levels
Sluggish intellectual ability

Inability to write well
Reduction in decision-making capacity
Expense
Damage to physical health
Diminished quality of conversation
Damage to mental health (anxiety and paranoia etc.)
Reduction in productivity
Reckless stupid behaviour
Reduced life expectancy (could also be on a list of advantages in darker times)
Increased likelihood of accidents
Hangovers
Decreased capacity to be a good friend
Increased grumpiness
Reduction in ability to appreciate beauty
Weight gain
Retardation in emotional growth caused by being anaesthetised
Booze is a carcinogen

***

If you are lonely when you are alone, you are in bad company.

JEAN-PAUL SARTRE

DAYS 1 TO 5 OF ABSTINENCE

Though intellectually I understand that alcohol could only ever represent a futile effort at papering over the cracks of unsatisfactoriness, I also have to acknowledge there have been fun times. The drunken antics have been numerous. At one of my house parties – yes, I used to live in a house like civilised people – we gathered in the garage for the purpose of entertainment in the form of shooting a switched-on telly with a speargun. It got a lot of laughs. Bouncing around a field on a sofa cushion being towed behind a car – that was also a lot of fun. And have you ever tried electrocuting a pickled gherkin with 240 volts of electricity? The poor little green fellow glows, smokes and writhes like the victim of a gruesome execution by electric chair – a great party trick. I cringe to think how easily these drunken antics could have gone wrong – accidentally spearing more than the onscreen TV presenter, electrocuting myself or someone else instead of the gherkin. But though there has been drunken fun, when I think back, it's largely been a sham.

When I think about drinking I have a Pavlovian response and start salivating. What will I do in the evenings instead? Write to you perhaps. Reading *Man's Search for Meaning* by Nazi concentration camp survivor Victor Frankl I find the word psychohygiene. I think of its opposite, psychotoxin – that's what alcohol has become for me.

Under the yoke of alcohol, ideas which might have found their way into this writing were left stumbling around my neural cortex, stranded on the margins of consciousness in a quagmire of muddled thinking leaving me frustrated by my own mental sloth. Three days into not drinking and such thoughts are beginning to find an escape trajectory.

In *Man's Search for Meaning* Frankl describes how inmates in the Nazi concentration camps would try to talk each other out of suicide, often unsuccessfully. He found the most effective means of talking a person down was to focus on whatever gave a prisoner's life meaning – someone they loved and cherished, or perhaps an unfinished work of creativity which the prisoner would hope to finish once free.

Before becoming a prisoner Frankl had been a practising psychiatrist. In the intense conditions of the camps he used this knowledge to observe human behaviour. His observations led him to believe that *meaning* is a vital part of the human life-force, it's what provides the will to continue. He noted that once prisoners lost their life-meaning they soon perished, either from sickness or suicide.

When I think about my darkest moments, when I have felt as hopeless as a fish in a trawler's net, this is when I have lost touch with the meaning of my life. In the absence of children or a partner, I realise the swimming has become a source of meaning, where I reconnect body and soul.

Walking into my bedroom I notice the evening sun is illuminating the bottle of baby shampoo I use to clean my swim goggles. The bottle is glowing, its own yellow intensified by the sunlight. 'How beautiful,' I think. Then I realise that under the mental fog of alcohol I almost certainly wouldn't have noticed this.

To describe alcohol as an anaesthetic is more appropriate than I had realised. A basic definition of the word is *without perception*, but more subtly you can take it to mean *without the ability to appreciate beauty*. Without it in my system I realise what I've been missing. Yes that's right, free with every bottle of alcohol comes a pair of poo-tinted glasses.

DAY 6

Wake at 5.45 a.m. Breakfast, then to the beach to meet some swimmers for a seven o'clock swim. The sea remains at 11 °C but with the chilly morning air it feels colder. A 25-minute swim. Getting up at this hour after drinking the night before would have been horrible, possibly impossible.

My face is less bloated and flabby. The mind fog continues to reduce. Yesterday I cycled up a hill I've climbed many times. It felt easier. Perhaps life with alcohol is like driving a car with the handbrake on.

DAY 12

The Black Dog has reappeared. What the Sultans of Sobriety don't tell you is that without the Morpheus of alcohol, the pain, vulnerability, confusion, internal conflict and contradictions of human existence can become more clearly defined, cutting deeper into the heart.

Without swimming, this experiment in sobriety would already have been dead in the water. The sea temperature, which stayed at 11°C for a month, has suddenly gone up to 13°. Only a couple of degrees but it's noticeable and I'm now swimming without neoprene shorts, gloves or socks. I am surprised how much difference those garments make, even though they cover a comparatively small proportion of my body. Swimming without the neoprene, my privates feel the cold amniotic fluid of mother earth and my bare cold hands make me feel strangely vulnerable. All of this makes me feel alive.

DAY 14

The Grey Hound's sudden and unwelcome appearances have the ability to stop me in my tracks. On one occasion he arrived the day before a holiday. I didn't take the flight and spent a week in bed. Last summer the boat was booked into a boatyard to be taken out of the water for essential maintenance, but the Grey Hound turned up two days before and again I was unable to leave my bed for a week. Now, after last year's abortive attempt, I'm trying again, taking the boat on a two-day journey up the River Lea to a boatyard north of London, where I hope it will be finally be craned onto land.

North of London the Lea Valley is home to perhaps a hundred lakes. I stop overnight at Cheshunt and have an illegal swim. The lake has a spooky atmosphere; its water has a greasy feel and an unnatural blue tinge.

The Lea Valley Park Authority's bylaws ban many things you'd have thought people might enjoy doing in a park, including swimming. I don't get caught, but while I may sneer at over-zealous rule-makers, two days after my illegal swim a teenager tragically drowns in the same lake. No one knows how or why.

Scraping the weed and rust off the boat's bottom is hard work, but at the end of each day I am rewarded with an illegal swim in a different lake. I share the willow blossom-covered water with ducks, whose fear is equalled by their curiosity at this strange human splashing about in their domain.

Sleeping on the boat on dry land feels unnatural, but less so than staying personally dry. There's a small supermarket nearby, so buying booze would be easy. The urge to drink is almost overwhelming but somehow I manage to resist. Perhaps because I know drinking could sabotage the boat maintenance. A week later the boat is finished, and with fresh gleaming paint she looks better than she has in all the time I've owned her. Consequently she sells.

I feel a sense of satisfaction that I got the job done without being incapacitated by my four-legged nemesis. I'm beginning to think alcohol and the dog are in cahoots.

***

Men stumble over the truth from time to time, but most pick themselves up and run off as though nothing had happened.

WINSTON CHURCHILL

The vow of abstinence has protected me for a month. Now it's spent I feel vulnerable. Thanks to that month of sobriety the cultural and personal significance of alcohol have been at least partially uncloaked.

I am a man who in theory doesn't like bullshit – but who has consumed barrel loads of the bullshit-inciting drug. Without it circulating in my system I feel different, as though I can trust myself. Productivity has soared. The folds of face-flab have decreased. Unexpected things have occurred, such as my beard growing thicker and faster. Strangely my tolerance to cold water has decreased.

From the hernia operation I know that when you are put to sleep by anaesthetic you cease to experience a conscious world; you therefore don't experience the anaesthetic. I now understand that I was unknowingly living in a constant state of alcoholic anaesthesia. Unable to experience its effect because I was permanently under its yoke. My reality was marinated. It doesn't feel so much like an arrival, but rather that a new journey can begin to begin.

There have been lows during this month, and without alcohol there's been nowhere to run. Not drinking has shown me that habituated drinking is running. Having got through a month without booze my instinct is to celebrate by drinking. I resist the urge. But I know I'm not free of the intoxicant's grip.

I now acknowledge my pattern of turning to alcohol not only in moments of stress, but also at times of celebration, and as a reward for just getting through the day. All times are a time to drink. There's always a reason to do so. Am I an alcoholic? If that means alcohol adversely affects my life and has the capacity to continue to so, and that it's difficult or impossible to stop, then the answer is yes. This is the first time I have acknowledged that fact.

During the alcohol years, and that's most of them, I assumed a booze-free life would be the same as when I stopped drinking for a couple of days – that is, not very different to a life with alcohol. I hadn't realised that the psychoactive properties of long-term drinking take weeks, perhaps months, to ebb away. For the time being the urge to drink has shrunk to manageable proportions and I can now see that the benefits of sobriety outweigh the escapism of nightly drinking.

I am a man who has stumbled across a truth and have picked myself up. The question is, will I run off as though nothing has happened? The honest answer . . . I don't know.

***

While there's life, there's hope.

MARCUS TULLIUS CICERO

The sea continues to work its magic. In it I feel obliterated, yet this time not in a bad way. Not by shit, but rather by the enormity and wildness of the ocean. I share this boundaryless domain with billions of other creatures, some of which bite and sting. There are currents, waves and eddies. Sometimes l swallow water and choke and cough. Conditions are never the same and to survive it's necessary to adapt. There is discomfort. You have to use skill and strength, but you also have to know your limits. In the act of swimming, especially in the sea, you are working moment by moment to affirm your will for life.

Even when feeling depressed to the point of not being bothered if one is alive or dead, the *will to life* can remain strong. That's not a contradiction, the will-to-live is what stops most depressives, including myself, killing themselves. In swimming, as opposed to sinking, you exercise that will. For me this is one of the psychic ingredients of open water swimming. It's an affirmation, a proof to self of the will to life.

OVERESTIMATED

Before you can break out of prison, you must realise you are locked up.

UNKNOWN, quote on addiction

I've begun a six-day beach lifeguards' course in Hastings. I've always been slightly deaf and this week I'm feeling the same frustration I felt at school over not being able to hear and consequently understand what's going on in the classroom. Previously, including at school, I'd have dealt with these feelings of frustration by drinking in the evenings, which would have led to a negative feedback loop of poor performance and anxiety.

The lifeguard training is physically demanding, with sessions in pool and sea culminating in various tests: run 200 metres, enter the sea, swim 200 metres, rescue a casualty, return them to shore, then once back on land run another 200 metres. And in the pool swim 25 metres under water then 25 metres on the surface, before a timed 200-metre sprint on land. Completing the course while drinking at night would most likely have been impossible. Reflecting on this makes me think of what my life might have been like had I not been a drinker. I would have achieved a lot more, that's for sure.

All those empty bottles are flotsam and jetsam on the shoreline of my life. I imagine them littering a beach, there are thousands of them. They symbolise decades of wasted time. It feels good to be on parole from prison alcohol.

On the lifeguard course my own Battle of Hastings was the final test of getting an unconscious mock casualty, a limp fellow student, up a steeply sloping shingle beach, which was like attempting to carry a bag of cement up an incline covered with ball bearings. With practice, and luckily without herniating ourselves, all the students succeeded.

In theory I now have the knowledge to rescue a person in difficulty in the water. But I still dread such a situation.

***

'I panicked for a few seconds and that's when I remembered the radio commercial that told me to float instead of fighting the water. I just lay back and started floating and kicking my legs. Eventually, after about 20 minutes, I managed to get back to the safety of the beach. It saved my life.'

SURVIVOR of a near drowning, quoted on the RNLI website

Coincidentally, during the lifeguard course Hastings town was turned into a media circus by the inquests on seven people who had drowned in two incidents the previous summer a few miles east at Camber Sands. In one case a weak swimmer got into trouble, another beach goer went to their rescue, things didn't go to plan and they both drowned. A few weeks later, on the morning of 24 August, five young friends set off from London for a day on the beach at Camber. After parking their car they went out onto the sands and into the sea to play volleyball. It was a perfect summer's day.

Amy Wood, a 17-year-old surfer, thought she saw them in the water waving. But she was busy trying to help another swimmer in difficulty, and anyway she couldn't tell if they were playing or in trouble. The next time the five friends were seen was when their bodies washed up on the beach causing widespread panic.

The sands at Camber may look flat at low tide but are in fact undulating. As the tide rises, water creeps its way over the sand into the low points creating channels with strong currents, in which a person can easily find themselves out of their depth. There were some 25,000 people on the beach that day, but no one saw the five friends drown. The coroner in Hastings criticised the local council for not having provided a lifeguard service and gave a verdict of death by misadventure.

A few years ago I was talking to a friend's kid about water safety. I was concerned she could fall off my boat into the river. This ten year old wasn't taking me seriously. When I asked why, she told me she had learned to swim at school. I couldn't convince her that swimming in cold water, in clothes, in a river, isn't the same as swimming in a warm pool. The conversation got me thinking that teaching children to swim a length or two in a pool and giving them hearty congratulations for doing so might be similar to telling to a new driver, 'Now you've passed your driving test you don't have to worry about being involved in a road accident.'

***

Some decades ago, on holiday in France, I was windsurfing on a lake large enough to have half-metre-high waves kicked up by a strong summer wind. I wasn't wearing a buoyancy aid. I fell off and lost contact with the board, which was being blown away from me faster than I could swim after it. I was surprised how quickly I tired, and because of the waves I began choking. I'd been under and bobbed up again. I was panicking and certain I was about to drown when I saw my friend Chris windsurfing straight for me. I wasn't sure if I could stay afloat until he reached me. I was praying he didn't fall off his board. I stayed afloat and he didn't fall. I was saved, but it was horribly close. I had nightmares about this for years afterwards. I had overestimated my swimming ability based on my school-pool-congratulatory-swim.

A friend from our community of boaters was d chores inside her boat with her four year old playin deck. The cabin door was open. She had heard noth ner boy for a few minutes so she went to check on him. He was nowhere to be seen. She looked down into the water and was horrified to see the child sitting on the riverbed a metre and a half underwater. She dived in and pulled him out. He was fine. The boy hadn't made a splash when he entered the water and didn't cry for help. He had learned to swim in a pool. She had overestimated her son's ability to swim. If the river water hadn't been clear that day he would almost certainly have died.

According to the World Health Organisation's *Global Report on Drowning* (2015):

Every hour of every day more than 40 people around the world lose their lives to drowning. Whether it's small children slipping unnoticed into a pond, pool or well; adolescents swimming under the influence of alcohol or drugs; passengers on vessels that capsize; or residents of coastal communities struck by floods, the daily toll is a leading global killer and continues its quiet rise.

The young friends who died at Camber were described as competent swimmers. But what does that mean? That they could swim a length or two in a heated pool with no current or waves? The inquest was told that the sea temperature that day was about 12 °C, cold for the time of year and easily cold enough to have produced cold-shock.

If you are unaccustomed to being in water at 15 °C or less for the first couple of minutes, you are likely to experience cold-shock. During this time the gasp reflex means it will be impossible to control your breathing. If there are waves splashing water over your mouth or your mouth is submerged you may start choking, ich in turn is likely to cause panic, and panic is likely to cause drowning. For the unacclimatised, cold water will also cause a sudden increase in blood pressure, putting anyone with a dicky heart at risk.

The Royal National Lifeboat Institute's advice on cold water immersion is to lie on your back and float for the minute or so it takes for the cold shock to pass, after which time you can control your breathing and start swimming. If you are dressed your clothes are likely to have air trapped in them, which can give you some buoyancy, at least until the cold-shock has passed.

***

The physiology of cold water immersion was studied by the Nazis, who wanted to estimate the likely survival times of their sailors and airmen whose aircraft had ditched, or whose ships had been sunk. You can imagine their mode of operation. They had a plentiful supply of unwilling subjects for their experiments. But as well as being cruel, the Nazis were bad scientists. Survival outcomes in cold water vary with differing physiologies, mentalities, clothing, local conditions, and experience. The victims of their experiments were physically and mentally stressed and quite likely malnourished. The data produced is therefore unreliable.

The opposite of those Nazis are the likes of the beachgoer at Camber who went into the water to rescue a drowning person, without thinking of their own safety, and who drowned themselves.

***

Identifying a drowning person may not be easy, because they will often not call for help and may not raise their arms. Their body is likely to be vertical in the water with their head back.

Speed of response is important as there can be as little as twenty seconds before a drowning person goes under. If you come across a person in difficulty in water, the best course of action is to throw something to them which floats, or use a pole which they can grasp. If you enter the water to rescue them, take something with you which floats – otherwise you could both end up dead.

A drowning person is likely lock onto their would-be rescuer, pushing them underwater. On the lifeguard course we learned how to escape such death grips by pushing ourselves down under water and away from the drowning person. The theory is that they will only cling onto somebody above water and will therefore let go as soon as you submerge yourself.

***

Many of the people I know who live on boats, including myself, have rescued drowning people. One man I pulled out of the river was off his head on drugs; another had been punched into the river by muggers. In July 2015 police officers from the Territorial Support Group chased a 17-year-old boy with mental health problems into the river near my boat. This was clearly not a case of failing to identify a drowning person. It can't even be said to be an example of a botched rescue, because there was no attempt at rescue. Witnesses report that the police response 'lacked urgency'. It took the boy around four minutes to drown, while at least ten police officers looked on. One police officer said he believed the submerging boy was 'attempting to escape'.

Only some minutes after the boy went under for the last time did an officer go into the river, by which time it was too late and his body couldn't be found in the murky water. The body was later recovered by divers. The police also prevented members of the public going in to rescue the youngster. This makes me wonder if a beach lifeguard course should be mandatory training for police officers.

When I spoke to people in our community who witnessed the incident, I got the impression they were traumatised by what they'd seen. At the time of writing this tragic case is still the subject of investigation by the Independent Police Complaints Commission.

***

They who say that we should love our fellow-citizens but not foreigners, destroy the universal brotherhood of mankind, with which benevolence and justice would perish forever.

MARCUS TULLIUS CICERO

I decide to go and have a look at Camber Sands for myself. Rita, a friend from London, comes along for the day trip. After a two-hour ride from Brighton, the motorbike breaks down entering Camber's car park. After some ineffectual efforts to fix it I decide the beach is the best place to figure out how to deal with the situation – probably a truth for any problem.

Walking out between shops piled high with inflatable crocodiles and other brightly coloured beach paraphernalia we are greeted by square miles of light grey sand exposed by the ebbing tide. In the distance, to the west, the mouth of the River Rother, to the east Dungeness, and behind the beach grassy dunes. The sky is cloudless and there is a cooling onshore breeze, preventing children mounted on their inflatable apex predators from being blown out into English Channel.

The ethnic background of Camber's visitors was noted at the inquest, which commented that many of its day-trippers are from ethnic minorities, who according to a 2015 Swim England survey are half as likely to be able to swim as other British people, and some minorities may wear clothes into the sea for religious or cultural reasons. Clothes are not conducive to effective swimming. The group of friends who died here last summer were all of Tamil origin.

I love meeting and talking to people of different cultures and hearing their views on life. We aren't disappointed by the cultural mix on the beach – including ourselves. Rita is a mix of Asian and Irish and I have a great-great-grandmother with the name Gold, which I assume means Jewish ancestry.

There are thousands of people on the beach, but because of its vast size it isn't crowded. We head for a spot where people look like they're having most fun. We settle down for a picnic near a group of perhaps a hundred and fifty people of African origin. I chat with one of them. They are from London on their church's annual day trip and they're in party mood, well equipped with sound system, tables, chairs, picnic and BBQ apparatus. Teenagers from their group have escaped parental supervision and are boozing behind a shed at the back of the beach, the girls practising twerking, while younger kids are playing together in the sand, and grownups are in serious conversation solving the world's problems.

Next to the church group are fifteen or twenty people of Colombian origin, one of whom has lived for the last twenty-two years a stone's throw from where I once lived in London. We had almost been neighbours. She's complaining about the increase in violent crime in London and how unsafe she feels.

Next to the Colombians are a group of people of Turkish origin. One of them, a man in his mid-twenties, is digging a hole in the sand. He's about a metre and a half down. I think about the non-functional motorcycle and consider asking him to dig a hole for me to bury my head in.

Our lifeguard teacher surprised us rookies when he told us of the dangers of beach digging. People have been buried alive when their own beach excavations have collapsed in on them, while as the tide rises their holes are covered by water, meaning that people can fall into them out of their depth. I ask how deep he plans to dig. 'I'm going to China,' he replies.

'I hope it doesn't collapse in on you before you get there,' I say tactfully, in the hope he'll stop burrowing. Which he does.

My phone rings. The breakdown assistance has arrived so we walk back to the car park. Rita isn't a swimmer, so I leave her with repairs underway and head back to the beach on my own.

It's low tide and there is half a kilometre of sand between me and the water's edge. Even when I reach it I have to wade out few hundred metres before the water is deep enough to swim.

From the sea looking inland behind the sand dunes I can see a wind farm, and to the east Dungeness nuclear power station. Interesting juxtaposition of technologies, I think. Wind power predates nuclear by a long chalk, but it's only recently that wind is rivalling nuclear in the amount of electricity generated.

***

Dungeness is fuelled by uranium pellets. Imagine you take a load of these pellets out of their reactor and pile of them up in a field. You then place the fastest sprinter on earth behind a lead shield 100 metres from the pile. The starting gun goes off, the lead shield is raised, and the runner accelerates towards the pile of uranium. For a few seconds all looks well, but then they stagger and fall. The radiation dose has killed them before they reach the fuel pellets. Uranium has a half-life of 780 million years.

Dungeness is built on the coast so that sea water can be used as a cooling medium. A hundred million litres of it are extracted and returned to the sea 12 °C warmer every hour. The sea felt warm that day and I couldn't help wondering if I was experiencing uranium-warmed water. I also wondered if I was being exposed to radiation from the leaking pipe they missed during their last safety check. But of course *They* would never let such a thing occur, because *They* are infallible and never make mistakes. Which is exactly what *They* thought about Fukushima before its reactors exploded.

Sixteen years ago I was in the Polygon region of Kazakhstan, where the Soviets, a different *They,* carried out above-ground nuclear weapons tests which left behind huge blast craters. These crater creators experimented using nuclear bombs as a means of making dams and reservoirs. The theory must have been that a nuclear bomb would save all that fiddling about with earth-moving machines. Perhaps digging by nuclear weapon and beach burrowing are driven by the same primal instinct. Though with excavation by nuclear weapon you don't just get a little hole which could bury you alive, you get a whole radioactive lake.

As a publicity stunt a Soviet government minister actually swam in one of these lakes. Maybe I'm crazy as well for swimming near Dungeness, especially as I am someone who doesn't trust *They.* But how far is far enough from a nuclear reactor? Being on the same planet as Fukushima's breached reactors is less than desirable.

Fukushima is another word with words within. The *Fuk u* part being the attitude of the Japanese government, and *shima* the Japanese for island, in this case the Japanese island of Honshu, on which the Fuk u shima power plant stands. But the *shima* part isn't really accurate, as radioactive nuclides don't have an island mentality.

It's a twenty-minute swim out to and around an orange buoy. After the deaths at Camber, the beach now has two well-equipped and well-staffed lifeguard stations run by the RNLI. As I swim out I think I can feel their binoculars on me.

I return to the motorbike to find the breakdown guy has done a temporary fix, enough for us to ride back to Brighton. If only emotional breakdowns were that easily sorted. The motorbike carries us back to Brighton where I can do a permanent repair on the machine and will continue to carry out emotional maintenance on myself.

KARATE

The thing we learn from history is that we fail to learn from history.
HEGEL

One year they couldn't get me in the sea, the next they couldn't get me out. The year they couldn't, my sister, ten years older, and her friend, dragged me screaming, by my arms and legs, into the water, so my mum tells me. Surprisingly that experience didn't put me off, because the following year they couldn't get me out of the sea and had to drag me in the opposite direction. Rita and I are on a day trip to West Wittering beach, the first place I ever swam in the sea aged six.

Returning to this beach, and to my nearby childhood home, my memories are hazy, covered by the patina of time. Mum and Dad had made a bit of cash and status was important to them. It wasn't an objective I shared. Their aspirations of aristocracy didn't stick. I was more ragamuffin than royal. My behavioural problems were an embarrassment and undermined the image they wished to portray. I must have been a constant source of stress for them. What do you do with a child who can't concentrate in the concentration camp of school, won't conform, and can't read or write properly? The answer – send him to a psychologist. It was already too late, and the visit to the shrink only served to confirm an early self-realisation that there was something wrong with me.

Rita and I are outside the house I lived in as a child. My mind is taken back to a moment nearly half a century ago. The Beatles are world famous, hippies roam the streets (but never in this village), and the Cold War is at its height. My dad and I are in the living room, where I see a British soldier, his mouth covered by a white cloth, driving a bulldozer pushing mounds of decomposing bodies into mass graves. Shocked, the thirteen-year-old me asks my dad why?

The images on the TV documentary came from the liberation of concentration camps at the end of the Second World War. Hell on earth had been caught on camera and was being delivered into our living room. As the corpses were dozed their arms and legs made stiff involuntary flailing movements, as unnatural and forced as the ending of their lives.

The overwhelming number of corpses and the outbreak of disease meant there wasn't time to give them a dignified burial. The liberators were forced into batch-processing their disposal just as the Nazis had batch-processed their incarceration and murder. I may have been shit at school but seeing those images was a proper education, which created in me a need to find out more about our relationship with authority, a relationship which still fascinates and troubles me.

***

'The experiment requires that you continue,' says a lab-coat wearing authority figure to an unknowing subject of Stanley Milgram's 1963 obedience experiment. The subjects don't know they are the focus of an experiment. They have answered a newspaper advert and believe they are taking part in research into in learning. They don't know that the electric shocks they are instructed to administer are false, and that it is an actor screaming behind a screen as they up the fake shock level on the fake instrument console to a fake life-threatening 460 volts. The actor pretends he has a heart condition and eventually goes quiet, feigning death. The subjects have been told the research is to determine if the application of pain as punishment is an effective aid to learning. The real aim of the experiment is to see how many people will obey the authority figure and turn the shock level up to 'fatal'. The experimenters were expecting a 99.9 per cent refusal rate. The results were truly shocking – only 35 per cent of subjects refused to obey.

***

My plan is to swim in the place I first swam in the sea, and take a look around the places I knew as a kid. I hadn't connected this return to my childhood home with that moment in front of the TV, but the memories come flooding back. Seeing that film footage so early in life did a lot to shape who I am. It's why, combined with the fact I was beaten, intimidated and humiliated by an abusive headmaster at primary school, I still find it difficult to trust authority.

I recently learned that the same headmaster is alleged to have sexually abused children in his care. He was investigated by police, but he died before any charges were brought. It was while at this school that the depression started and it's been with me ever since. In the logic of a child after they sent me to that school I never fully trusted my parents again, even though they were oblivious to the abuse.

I didn't know it at the time, but those childhood experiences made me into what I would later learn is called an anarchist. The *an* in anarchy means without, and *archy* means leader. You could say anarchy is the opposite of monarchy (one leader). In popular culture the word has been degraded to mean a state of violent chaos. This couldn't be further from the political theory, which is the antithesis to Nazism, which imposes a strict hierarchy through force. Anarchy on the other hand would create order by consent and cooperation. A utopian dream? Perhaps. Some believe that Jesus was an anarchist.

***

My childhood home village of Itchenor is, in that traditional English village kind of way, a safe, comfortable and attractive place, (second) home to holders of capital who have benefited from a certain system of distribution. The village's main thoroughfare is a dead end terminating at the picturesque Chichester Harbour. But the place isn't only a physical cul de sac, to me it also feels like a cultural one – dull and lifeless. Just as when I was a kid, many of its cutesy, well-maintained houses are second homes. It wasn't my kind of place fifty years ago. It still isn't.

As Rita and I ride out of the village I feel a confusion of emotions. Nostalgia is mixed with sadness for that small boy that was me. A toe-curling shame that I haven't made peace with my past, and a sense of wasted years.

Next we head for West Wittering Beach. Approaching it we see its car park is on the scale of an international airport parking facility. At its entrance a large dot-matrix sign orders visitors to 'swim between the red and yellow flags' (where there is a lifeguard service). Parking is eight quid a day but they let us park the motorbike for free.

Eight quid multiplied by thousands of cars, that's a lot of money, but you can see why the place is so popular. The beach is made up of fine light grey sand backed by dunes, with far-reaching views over the Solent to the hills of the Isle of Wight, and across the mouth of Chichester Harbour to Hayling Island.

In 1951 West Wittering car park, its beach and the surrounding land were nearly sold to Butlins, who wanted to turn it into a holiday centre. But the residents of its nearby millionaire mansions fought the plan, and as the site included a profitable car park it was eventually sold as a self-sustaining business. Today it's called the West Wittering Estate PLC, whose stated objectives include 'the preservation of the beach and waters . . . for the safe and peaceful enjoyment of the public and the preservation of the rural and undeveloped nature'. Such are the contradictions of human affairs that a car park should bankroll the preservation and undeveloped nature of a place.

***

The car park industry was one I understood from an early age. In summer a grassy field in Itchenor was turned into a car park. At peak times it was staffed by a man in a little hut. At other times the car park was still used but the man wasn't there. All we had to do was place a sign in the window saying 'put money in slot'. The slot was already there. We put a box underneath it and would come back at the end of the day and collect the loot. A perfect crime. It was my friend Henry's idea – quite an impressive scam for an eleven year old. I would imagine Henry has made a ton of money in his life. I was a couple of years younger and nowhere near as savvy. Luckily the Great West Itchenor Car Park Scam didn't develop into further thieving, probably because the only time I got whacked by my dad was when the caper was discovered.

Naked photos of Henry's mum adorned their living room walls. They were arty types from London. Their house in Itchenor was one of those second homes, meaning Henry's visits were infrequent. Which is why our friendship did little to relieve my loneliness.

Henry was bolder than me. His dad had a shotgun. One time when his parents were out, which was always, we fired it into the field at the back of his house. The recoil nearly knocked me over and the noise was deafening.

There was an unbounded freedom in my childhood. Amateur

bomb making and guns were repeating themes. I even managed to shoot myself in the lip with my own airgun. Sensible careers advice for my younger self, semi-literate, and with a keen interest in explosions and firearms, would have been to join the army, or take up a career in armed robbery. But the military turned me down, probably not a bad thing as I don't have a stomach for blood, which means bank heists were out as well. What with my hopeless career development I should have taken more notice of the aphorism:

> *Give a man a fish, and feed him for a day. Teach a man to fish, and feed him for a lifetime.*

But years later as an adult I figured out a more accurate maxim . . .

> *Give a man a gun and he can rob a bank. Give a man a bank and he can rob the world.*

***

West Wittering Beach is on the eastern side of the mouth of Chichester Harbour. There are often dangerous currents at harbour entrances and West Wittering is no exception. Even the untrained eye can see an eddy fence, where water running out of Chichester Harbour meets water flowing along the English Channel. Swim out too far and you'll likely be swept away down the Solent.

Thousands of people are packed onto the beach near the car park. We're surprised to see a group of fifty people in the shallows dressed in karate suits sparring with each other. They are from a martial arts club in Guildford. A party of people of Chinese origin are playing football, while Russian and Eastern European languages can be heard. As at Camber, Britain's diversity is an audible and visible feature of the beach. From turbans, saris and shalwar kameez, to the Japanese art of karate, the international influences on British culture are evident. This was not the case the first time I came to this beach half a century ago, when there was no lifeguard service either.

Give a lifeguard a loudhailer and he'll make a lot of noise. Give a man an open beach and he'll walk away from the loudguards' lifehailing. Rita and I head east away from the hubbub where we soon find ourselves in peace and alone. The current is flowing east and so I swim westward at a relaxed pace, remaining geostationary. I'm in the water for twenty minutes and come out thinking how all those twenty minutes eventually add up to half a century, and it feels like the blink of an eye.

The motorbike carries Rita and me home safely, evidence that I've made a reasonable job of repairing it. But it's an old machine and I'm well aware it's likely to break down again. Pretty much like me.

RUBBISH

There comes a point where we need to stop just pulling people out of the river. We need to go upstream and find out why they're falling in.

DESMOND TUTU

When I was seven my dad and I swam in the River Rhine. That evening we both went down with the mother of all diarrhoea and vomiting. It's that experience that first left me uneasy about swimming in rivers.

Two years later, back in England I watched as an aeroplane swooped low over my head and across the lake, heading towards a rolling field of wheat. Then, abruptly, engine roaring, it climbed, banked, turning through 180 degrees, throttling back and descending, heading directly back towards me for another low pass over the field, repeating the manoeuvre over and over. Standing by Birdham Pool, the nine-year-old me marvelled at this daredevil flying.

The following day, bicycling about feeling lonely, I returned to the same place. Half a century on I still have a clear memory of what I saw. Floating upside-down were thousands of silver fish, all dead. The aircraft had been spraying pesticide.

About the same age, I was aboard a cross-Channel ferry. A crew member appeared through a door, walked across the deck and upended a rubbish bin over the side of the ship, then disappeared back through the same door. I couldn't believe my eyes. 'Dad, what's that man doing?'

'He's dumping rubbish, son.' The lack of surprise in my dad's voice obviously meant this was normal behaviour in the adult world.

Given my knowledge of how fond humans are of dumping unwanted waste into rivers, it's surprising I let my enthusiasm to swim across the Thames cloud my judgement. I realise that the Port of London Authority's ban on swimming is a red herring. The issue is contamination, not consent. Common sense has reasserted itself in the form of research. I've signed up with Thames Water to receive email alerts whenever they discharge untreated sewage into the river. Those emails drop into my inbox every time there's heavy rain. In 2013 three hundred swimmers became sick after an organised swimming event in the Thames, and despite pre-emptive antibiotics celebrity swimmer David Walliams became ill swimming in the Thames. Somehow I've erased from my memory the bacterial infection which embedded itself in the skin of my legs after I carried out maintenance on my boat on the Thames riverbank near Isleworth. Having lived on a boat on the River Lea I know how filthy its water is. And it's a tributary of the Thames, debouching upstream of Gallions Reach where I was planning to swim.

If the Port of London Authority were serious about stopping people swimming in their river all they need do is tell the truth about pollution, but strangely internet searches return countless articles claiming the river is clean. One website states, 'The Thames is cleanest river in the world that runs through a major city.' It's the sub-clause which gives the sentence a whiff of truthiness. A comparable description of a swimming pool might read . . . 'the cleanest in the world, compared with other pools containing fecal matter'. Then there are chemical contaminants and the bodily fluids drained from human corpses by undertakers and anything else which finds its way into the sewers. I must have been crazy to consider immersing myself in the fetid waters of the Thames.

***

Moving to Brighton has not only meant swapping cities. I've also swapped polluters, from Thames to Southern Water, who were recently fined £126 million for contaminating the sea and rivers along the south coast. Rachel Fletcher, chief executive of Ofwat, the regulator which set the fine, says, 'What we found in this case is shocking. In all, it shows the company was being run with scant regard for its responsibilities to society and the environment. It was not just the poor operational performance but the coordinated efforts to hide and deceive customers of the fact that are so troubling.' Southern Water's behaviour doesn't shock me. I see this as normal behaviour for corporations. What's unusual is that they got caught.

Southern Water's latest scam may be dumb, but at least it has comedy value. No, they aren't going to stop bears shitting in the woods, no one would be that stupid. Their strategy is to stop seagulls shitting in the sea.

After the Ofwat fine Southern Water got caught in another scam to prevent the already critical bacteria levels in the sea at Worthing tipping them into back into the fine-zone. As seagull poo is rich in bacteria, they hired a company with hawks to patrol Worthing seafront to scare off the airborne defecators. A halt was put to this after they were reported to the police for harassing herring gulls, which are a protected species.

This week in Brighton and Hove, heavy rain has led to the discharge of raw sewage, and the outflow from 'rainwater' gullies has left huge mile-long dark slicks of filth in the sea. Neither the lifeguards nor the seafront office displayed warning signs; consequently people were swimming in the putrescence. This is normal after heavy rain, so I avoid swimming in the sea after a downpour, and I've now decided not to swim in rivers at all because it's impossible to know what's in them. Of course all river water ends up in the sea, but the ocean is big so that pollutants are diluted.

Picture this. I'm walking up a small backstreet in Brighton. A distressed baby herring gull, almost adult sized, is flapping about in the middle of the road. Perhaps its first flight off a nearby roof didn't go according to plan. A taxi full of passengers drives slowly past me and over the top of the bird. After an eternity, the gull reappears. Though flustered, with its wings at an awkward angle, it's remarkably still three-dimensional. Without so much as a backwards glance the taxi continues. Another metaphor, but also a true representation of our species' relationship with the planet and its ecology. My alter ego, an alien, sends a memo back home to my handler on a far distant planet. "Humans: seldom in the history of life in the universe has any species evolved such intelligence and then so entirely wasted it."

Only kidding I am really human, and being such is disconcerting because that means I'm a hypocrite. Even small tasks, like oiling my bicycle and doing laundry, become significant when multiplied by seven billion people. Waste water full of microplastic and detergent from millions of washing machines discharge down drains and eventually into the sea I love. I wash my clothes and drive a car, so I'm a co-conspirator.

I recently watched the *Kirkella*, a new 3,976 tonne, fossil fuel-guzzling factory fishing ship, cruising up the Thames. While most onlookers seemed happy to see her, the sight of it sent a shiver down my spine. The vessel is Grim Reaper to 15 million fish a year. Investment in this object compels its owners to plunder the ocean, if only to recover its running costs and pay for its construction. Multiply this financial imperative across many industries and you end up with the death cult called laissez-faire capitalism, whose purpose is to convert live things into dead things to make money.

According to Adam Smith, the messiah of capitalism, an invisible hand guides our economic activities ensuring that inefficiencies and mistakes are corrected by bankruptcies. Does an invisible hand not also guide life on earth? If so, how will it correct human mistakes and inefficiencies in the market place of the ecosystem?

By virtue of living I play a part in our culture's assault on the planet. But at least I have swimming as respite from the human game of apex predator and most significant polluter. In the sea I become part of the ecology. The tables are turned, I go from predator to potential prey. From polluter to potential victim of pollution.

HITLER

You can cut all the flowers but you cannot keep Spring from coming.
PABLO NERUDA

To the south-east is Gunfleet wind farm. To the west the distant form of Bradwell nuclear power station, its outline grey, angular and utilitarian. I have a sense of déjà vu with the nuclear and wind energy in close proximity. It's Camber Sands revisited, except this time Rita and I are on the beach in Jaywick in Essex. This settlement is supposed to be the poorest place in the UK. Poor in monetary terms maybe, but it has its own beach, which is something many would pay top dollar for.

Developer Frank Stedman watched with interest as Charles Nevil turned a profit selling plots of land in Peacehaven. In 1928, believing he could replicate Nevil's business model in Jaywick, Stedman sold small plots of land on which East Londoners could build their own holiday homes. The plots sold for as little as £25. Since then Jaywick has been through the ebb and flow of fortune. Today it's struggling.

The village is comprised mostly of small, poorly maintained homes. The community is blighted with high unemployment and is one of few places in the country with sensibly priced housing, the opposite of West Wittering with its billionaire mansions. I see suffering etched into many of the faces. Yet one thing Jaywick has, that many more affluent neighbourhoods don't, is a sense of community, which is apparent in the friendly way locals all greet each other.

On the settlement's curved beach is a wrecked yacht covered with low-quality graffiti, which provides a practical demonstration of the law of unintended consequences, as it is now an unofficial adventure playground satisfying local kids' yearning to be pirate captains. The same law made Adolf Hitler a better provider of children's play areas than the borough councils of the metropolis, with the post-blitz bomb sites becoming unofficial adventure playgrounds for the children of east London.

Jaywick's beach is made up of a mixture of sand and pebbles, backed by small grassy dunes. The beach slopes at a pleasing angle into the sea. The water here tastes less salty than on the south coast, and I feel slightly less buoyant. Money has been spent on flood defences, not only on the seawall but also on large breakwaters consisting of huge boulders of granite which I can see breaking the surface during my twenty-minute swim. I wonder why money hasn't been spent on fixing the village's potholed roads.

From the beach we take in the view. The distant shape of Bradwell nuclear power station makes me think of the theft of twenty uranium fuel rods from the plant. I wonder what really happened.

***

It was 1966, the psychic wounds of the Holocaust still fresh. Ten years previously Israel had sided with the British and French to take control of the Suez Canal; consequently relations between Egypt and Israel's other Arab neighbours had soured. The new state of Israel, barely two decades old, was feeling threatened. There was a strong motivation for Israel to develop its own nuclear 'deterrent'. Consequently Israeli agents had been paying close attention to the UK's nuclear programme. They were surprised by the lack of security surrounding Britain's nuclear fuel.

It takes years to refine and concentrate fissile material, and the Israelis were making slow progress. While France was providing Israel with nuclear technology, it monitored the transfer of nuclear fuel closely, leaving little opportunity for sleight-of-hand transfers.

In 1966 there was no wind farm off the Jaywick coast, but Bradwell nuclear power station would have looked the same as it does today. From Jaywick beach you'd have been too far away to see Arthur Sneath, a worker at the plant, creeping into Bradwell's fuel store and stealing twenty Magnox fuel rods. Nor would you have seen his accomplice Denis Hadley driving off in a van loaded with their loot. This nuclear fuel was different to that used in Dungeness, which is why the alleged thieves would not have been irradiated to death.

The rods were supposedly recovered when a police patrol car randomly noticed Hadley's van had defective steering. They stopped the van and discovered the fuel rods. The official story is that Sneath and Hadley were planning to sell the rods for scrap, though I personally have never heard of a scrap yard which takes radioactive fuel rods.

The Bulletin of Atomic Scientists lists this breach in security at Bradwell as 'obscure'. A strange word to use. It makes me wonder if its author also had doubts over the validity of the official story. It's impossible to know what really happened, but my money is on the Israelis.

The loss of radioactive material is surprisingly common. Six more Magnox fuel elements went missing in North Wales in 1972. And, again in 1966, the Americans accidentally dropped three nuclear bombs on the sleepy fishing village of Palomares in southern Spain, and lost another one in the sea nearby, though they claimed to have found it four months later. Luckily the three bombs dropped on the village didn't go critical. I found out about the lost American bomb only after I'd been swimming nearby in the 1990s. Many locals don't believe the fourth bomb was ever recovered.

Looking out from Jaywick beach, the proximity of nuclear and wind energy makes me think of a centuries-long battle between species. First the invasive tentacles of the fossil fuel-powered steam engines strangulate the windmill and sailing ship. Then nuclear joins forces with fossil fuels and it looks as though the native wind will not survive. But gradually wind has fought back, plunging its roots into the earth. Until today, when wind turbines, solar and other sustainable forms of generation are sprouting up all over the place, gradually consigning nuclear to the radioactive waste repository of history, and fossil fuels to a museum curiosity.

TRUST

A ship is safe in harbour, but that's not what ships are for.
JOHN A. SHEDD

Nicky my swimming friend has her bicycle stolen. She goes to Mitch and Granddad, a small Brighton bike shop, to look at new bikes. Because I know about bicycles, she asks my advice and tells me about her conversation with Mitch, how knowledgeable and likeable he is.

Three weeks later Nicky still hasn't made her mind up about a new bike. It's Brighton Pride weekend. The parade isn't rained on. The sunny city is full to the gunwales with people dressed as they might like to every day, but mostly don't. Extravagant glittery makeup and brightly coloured spandex are everywhere.

Later that evening, while pubs, bars and clubs are fall of hedonists necking alcohol and hoovering white powders, a few miles west, at midnight, four friends leave Shoreham Harbour in a little motorboat called *James 2*. The party scene isn't their thing. They have fishing on their minds, and they know a good spot for mackerel a couple of miles offshore.

After motoring for twenty minutes they kill the engine and drift under a starry sky. The only sounds their jovial conversation, the whirring of fishing reels, and waves lapping against the hull. Soon they're catching mackerel. The four friends are happy and contented. Whisky, laughter and good conversation flow.

James 2's skipper goes into the cabin out of the 5 mph wind to roll and smoke a cigarette. A mile and a half away, against the shore lights, a boat can be seen leaving harbour. It's a commercial scallop fishing vessel called *Vertrouwen*. Her crew are in their bunks. The skipper is alone on the bridge. Using the autopilot he alters course slightly to port, heading south-east. *Vertrouwen* is now on a collision course with *James 2*. Its skipper is completing the departure log. He then sends a message to friend on Facebook.

The men in the cockpit of *James 2* see the dark outline of their stalker behind its dazzling deck lights. *James 2*'s skipper chucks his cigarette into the sea and tells his friends to reel in their lines. He starts the engine. In an attempt to make themselves visible, they shine their torches at the approaching vessel. It's much bigger than their little boat – and moving fast. It doesn't alter course.

James 2 makes a panicked turn. The little boat is carrying the four friends as fast as it can. A bit like the skipper of the *Princess Alice*, they make the futile effort of shouting up at the approaching wall of steel. It doesn't answer back, but continues ploughing through the water, pushing up a bow wave as high as their little fibreglass cruiser. *James 2* is caught a glancing blow and the bow wave breaks over the back of their boat, swamping it. The friends bail frantically, but it's futile. The difference between sea and boat is diminishing rapidly. They turn and look at the receding shape of their nemesis, and again shine their torches at it. It disappears into the night.

James 2 is heading for the seabed. In seconds they'll all be in the water. They look for anything that will float. One of them empties a fuel can, another uses his fishing knife to cut a fender from the side of the boat. He passes his knife to his friend who does the same. They swim clear as she goes down. It's suddenly very quiet and a long way to land.

The men quickly drift apart and lose sight of each other. But this isn't the sort of drifting which can happen when friends move to different cities. This is more final. They shout each other's names and 'Are you OK?' After twenty minutes there's only one voice left. And for that voice the silence is terrifying. It's a mile and a half to land and the shore lights look tiny. The clear starry sky only makes him feel more alone in the enormity of the universe. The fender under his arm is keeping him afloat, but it also impedes swimming. He's forced into a one-handed doggy paddle and makes little progress.

The water temperature is 16 °C. After an hour he is cold, after two hours he's colder. After three hours he's dizzy, disorientated and cold. He feels a sense of hope as the sky brightens to the east. Then it's dawn.

The rising sun is shining through the aft windows in the wheelhouse of a lobster fishing boat as it makes its way west along the south coast. Its crew are drinking tea and enjoying a few jokes. Their eye is caught by something in the water. They are surprised to see a figure frantically waving. They haul the hypothermic survivor aboard. He's been in the water for five hours and twenty minutes and can barely talk, but he manages to tell them his friends are still in the water. They make a Mayday call and a search and rescue operation begins.

Twenty minutes later I'm woken from a warm slumber by the sound of a helicopter. I open the curtains and see a red and white coastguard chopper flying to and fro out to sea. My friend Harry is staying the weekend. She says a prayer for whoever is in trouble at sea.

A couple of hours later I'm on the beach meeting the swimmers. We can see two identical rescue helicopters, and through the binoculars I can see perhaps fifteen boats parallel to each other, half a mile apart, slowly heading westwards. They are obviously searching. Some of the swimmers discuss what is happening while others say nothing. I instinctively understand. For those who remain silent the situation reminds them of their own mortality in the water.

After eight hours the search is called off with one body found. The two missing men are presumed dead. A few days later another body is discovered floating near the Rampion Wind Farm, which is still under construction. It isn't one of the two remaining friends. A few days later another body is discovered down the coast in Saltdean. This isn't one of the friends either.

***

The quantity of bodies floating around in the English Channel should not come as a surprise. There are far too many tragic drownings around our coastline. There are also those who deliberately end their own lives in the sea, some of whose bodies will never be found.

Eight days after the little boat went down the crew of a fishing boat spotted another body floating off Shoreham Harbour. The lifeboat which recovered the body found a second on their way back to base. These were the remaining two friends. All were now accounted for. Three dead, one survivor.

I have filled in the gaps between what I saw on the day and what was reported in the accident investigation. This is guesswork. The exact details will most likely never be known. According to the accident report, had the crews of both vessels been keeping an effective lookout the collision would never have happened. Had the crew of *James 2* been wearing life jackets they would all have survived. But it's easy to have hindsight. Foresight is far more useful, but that of course involves making sense of that most tricky of things – risk.

The first thing the crew of *Vertrouwen* knew of the accident was when they were approached by marine accident investigators. The man who passed the knife to his friend, allowing him to cut a fender free, saved his life. Nicky won't be buying a bicycle from Mitch because it was his body they found the morning after the accident. The word *vertrouwen* means trust in Dutch.

***

Vices surround and assail men [and women] from every side . . . and do not allow them to discern the truth, but keep them overwhelmed and rooted in their desires.

SENECA

It's night. I see a strange scene. I'm on a dark urban street looking into a building. Through the window I see a man in a mind-altered state. The only source of light in the room comes from a candle. The man is drunk and careless, his bare arm in the flame. He doesn't realise he is being burned, but even if he did he wouldn't be bothered because he has achieved his objective. Alcohol has produced systemic indifference to misfortune, including his burnt arm. He is trapped in a state of confusion and indifference. Poor fellow. I look more closely at his face. Shock. He has my face. I wake up.

The decades have passed and I haven't fixed myself. What I've done instead is to tread water. Just about staying afloat in a lake of wine. Now I'm in the early stages of drowning in it. After the month of abstinence I started with the occasional drink. From this it's built up and until I've found myself drinking heavily again.

I've drunk because at times the emotional pain has been intense and any escape seemed desirable. As I look at the drinking habits of those around me I see the same drama being played out. I observe drinkers trying to make light of their alcohol use, insisting on how funny their bad behaviour was or how comical their hangover is. A sort of mock trench humour. Mock because it isn't funny.

***

It's no measure of good health to be well adjusted to a profoundly sick society.

KRISHNAMURTI

A bit like Arnold Schwarzenegger in the film *Terminator*, he's back and doing damage. I thought I had him tamed, but over the last couple of weeks he's gradually gnawed through his leash. The Schweinhund is sat here in the corner of the room radiating toxic energy. He's a strange foe. He doesn't bare his teeth. He's passive and silent, attributes which make him all the more sinister.

In an effort to keep him at bay I've exhausted myself with swimming, but when I get back onto land he's there waiting for me. I'm no longer living in London and have the good fortune to live in a beautiful home, yet still the Grey Hound, like a compulsive beach digger, is burrowing into my soul and burying his bone of discontent.

I often complain about our government who make only token gestures of making things better for ordinary folks, treating the symptoms rather than the causes of a sick society, but maybe I'm doing the same with myself. Depression is my symptom, which I was treating with alcohol and now with swimming. The problem is I can't identify its root cause.

LOCUSTS

The fishermen know that the sea is dangerous and the storm terrible, but they have never found these dangers sufficient reason for remaining ashore.

VINCENT VAN GOGH

The palms of my hands are sweating as I look up at the steep conifer-covered hillside rising from the opposite shore six hundred metres away. The evening sky is full of dark, ominous clouds. Wind is gusting down the glen, whipping up small waves on the loch. I ignore the feeling of dread and get in. My bare hands aren't sweating anymore, instead they ache with cold, but that soon subsides. The water temperature is perhaps 11 °C. I put my face down and start swimming in the knowledge there will be no rescue in this remote spot.

I feel uneasy looking down into the dark unknown depths, trying to keep monsters out of my mind. Halfway across I'm spooked by the strange sensation that the whole body of water, the entire loch, has moved like a seesaw. I stop and look around; everything seems normal. Just an overactive imagination. I continue. At the far side, the water is shallow. My legs and arms tangle in weed. Turning to look back the way I've come, it's just about possible to make out our green tent on the opposite side of the loch. It's a long way back. I begin the return journey and make landfall without molestation by monster. I feel a minor sense of achievement. There really wasn't anything to be scared of other than my own demons, and that includes the Grey Hound, who I have just outswum. Hopefully I've left him paddling round in circles tangled in weed on the far side of the lake, but I know he'll find his way back.

Our tent is pitched beside Loch Voil on a small raised promontory. The glen runs east–west and its northern flank, under which we are camped, is permanently damp and covered in sphagnum moss, nature's own wet wipe; useful when the toilet facilities are al fresco. Finding a discreet and private place, digging a small hole in which to make my deposit, I realise this is my Toilet of the Year, with magnificent loch views.

After supper cooked on a camping stove Rita and I sit and chat. I look at her beautiful face illuminated by the camp fire and feel lucky to be here in this gorgeous landscape with a good friend. The Grey Hound is still nowhere to be seen. He hates this kind of thing. His most recent visitation was such that it felt like I was falling into a bottomless pit, one I might not have been able to climb out of. But at least it was the motivating force to fulfil a decades-long wish to visit the Outer Hebrides. Loch Voil is on the way, and a place to stop and camp for the night.

The next day we continue north. Like a typical Sassenach, the first time I visited the Highlands I was expecting to find something just a little different to England. How wrong I was. The sparse population and rugged landscape quickly integrate themselves into the psyche, soothing a troubled mind, and the further from London we get the more humane the culture becomes.

Our wheels roll onto Skye Bridge and as we travel uphill towards its apex its name seems appropriate, because all we can see is sky and dramatic cloud formations. Rita and I debate if the place should still be considered an island now it's connected to the mainland by a bridge.

That evening on Skye the wind is whipping through our campsite, this time an official one which we are sharing with shiny motorhomes. Through their windows I see people watching flatscreen TVs. Their residents have every luxury. It looks a bit too comfortable. I return to our tent and its windblown flapping canvas for a bad night's sleep.

In the morning we head for Skye's Coral Beach. The Scots are apparently not immune to that great English tradition of calling things what they are not. The nearest coral is west of here, way out to sea beyond the continental shelf. The cream-coloured beach is made up of broken particles of dead seaweed. Dead Seaweed Beach. You can see why that name didn't stick. Poetry is more important than accuracy, especially in Scotland.

Rita and I park the car and walk a couple of kilometres along the coast. Close to shore, seals are basking in the bright sunshine on small rocky islands known as skerries. I don't know the currents, so I watch the water for a while before getting in, and then keep close to shore swimming parallel with the beach. I don't want to be swept out to sea in water this cold in a place where rescue would be a long time coming. The water is crystal clear, its turquoise tint contrasting perfectly with the cream-coloured sand. The air and the sea feel pure and that makes me feel the same. But Skye doesn't feel remote, which is probably down to that bridge.

Later that morning we continue north to Uig where we board the *Hebrides*, the ferry which plies the route to Tarbert on the Isle of Harris. It carries on average ninety cars; that's ten less than when she began service seventeen years ago. No, the ship hasn't shrunk. While roads have got busier and parking places harder to find, cars have got bigger. The car we're driving, a fifteen-year-old Nissan Micra, is the smallest vehicle on the ship, for which we didn't get a discount.

It's not only the size of cars that's increasing, so too is the number of visitors heading for Scotland's hitherto remote islands.

Without a hint of irony, an advisor in the Tarbert tourist office informed me that the increase in holidaymakers is 'like a plague of locusts'. She was referring to a weekend earlier in the summer when visitors to Skye reached record numbers and the island was gridlocked by dimwitted drivers using passing places on the single-track roads for parking. To accommodate increasing numbers of locusts and their escalating car size, the ferry operators have ordered a bigger ship which will carry 125 modern-sized cars.

The sea which separates the mainland from the Outer Hebrides is called the Minch. If you'd been around 1.2 billion years ago you'd have seen the mother of all firework displays when a massive meteorite collided with Earth and landed right there. Since then things have cooled down; the summer sea temperatures are unlikely to rise above 13 °C, which is why we are travelling by car, not by motorbike. The Micra may be small but it has a great heater.

The *Hebrides* manoeuvres into the small natural harbour of Tarbert. We are a long way from London and it feels like what goes on in the capital is irrelevant. This feeling is of course misleading.

The double place-name problem has followed us north. We are now on an island called Lewis and Harris. I never managed to establish why the island has two names, and couldn't figure out exactly where the boundary between Harris and Lewis is. But in simple terms, Lewis is to the north, Harris to the south.

The island is incised by sea and pockmarked by lochs, its landscape littered with ancient grey boulders covered with pastel-coloured lichen. Rocky outcrops are separated by beige sheep-grazed grass and heather. The rocks of the Outer Hebrides are amongst the oldest on the planet, formed around 3 billion years ago. Heat, pressure and friction over geological time have sculpted this landscape, carving out valleys, pushing up mountains and then wearing them down again. While the musculature of capitalism may be on show in the City of London's architecture, here you can feel the raw ancient power of Mother Nature and are left in no doubt who's going to win in the fight humans have picked with it. This is a showcase of elemental forces which puts not just a person, not only humanity, but the whole of existence into context. Perhaps that's why religion plays such an important role in Hebridean culture. You can forget buying anything on a Sunday, even petrol. All retail opportunities shut down.

This meeting point of land and Gulf Stream, with its moist Atlantic air, spawns changeable weather. If it's raining now, you know soon it won't be. If it isn't raining you know it soon will. It's a meteorologist's paradise with spectacular cloudscapes. The Hebridean climate is harsh. Salty air rusts all unprotected steel. Abandoned buildings are subjected to nature's reclamation and soon turned to ruins. The North Atlantic pounds the west coast with unforgiving waves and currents. A farmer on Harris told us that 100 mph winds occur every few winters.

Rita and I soon realise these islands are also a waveologist's paradise, because you can't go anywhere without being waved at. The roads are single track. Drivers travelling in opposite directions have to negotiate passing. The process requires an acknowledgement, which varies between a full-blown wave and the casual raising of an index finger from the steering wheel. Quite the opposite of driving in London, where different fingers are frequently raised with an entirely different sentiment.

Me, a modern human, I sit in the passenger seat of a machine powered by the juice of the same primal planetary forces that have created this landscape. Rita drives our little car west. I sit and take in the surroundings. It's a beautiful moment.

A while later on the road to Horgabost we meet our only aggressive driver of the trip. He – of course it's a he – approaches a passing place at speed, hogging the road and braking his large black 4x4 at the last moment, forcing us into a pothole. We don't feel well disposed towards him. He doesn't get a wave, and I only just manage to resist giving him the London finger.

We set up camp in a hollow in the dunes behind Horgabost Beach, because this offers some shelter from the almost constant wind. Though mentally wearing, the Hebridean wind has the advantage of grounding the midges. Who wins in a fight, human or midge? Correct answer, midge. Or to be accurate, midges. There are billions of them, and oh do they make your skin itch. From our pitch we have views across the bay to the kilometres-long white sand of Luskentyre Beach, with the hills of Taransay island a few miles offshore.

Here on the outer limits of the kingdom I've been feeling shit scared, as though each swim will be my last. This particular swim is convenient, right next to our tent, which is right next to the white sandy beach, yet when I enter the water the fear subsides only slightly. The fear increases again when I nearly swim into a compass jellyfish. It has long stinging tentacles. Trying without success to turn myself into a hovercraft, I pass a few centimetres above the mysterious creature. I may be un-stung, but I'm un-nerved. I swim on parallel with the beach. I get out feeling cold and thankful the ordeal is over, but I have to acknowledge it was worth it because there is the usual mood uplift. It's a short walk back to the tent for a hot cup of tea.

The nearest car exhausts and factory chimneys upwind of here are thousands of miles across the Atlantic. The sun's rays hit my retinas and bare skin and I can feel the air is as untainted by the products of hydrocarbon combustion as they can be in our era. This place is having an effect on me. Newfoundland and Labrador is the closest land mass across the ocean. Maybe the Grey Hound has left to be with his cousins on the other side of the Atlantic.

I swim in the same place the following morning. As get in I notice a boat approaching. It looks like a military landing craft. I figure it must now be used for fishing. I tread water and wait until it's moored. I will have to swim around it. I'm keen to avoid being minced by the vessel's propeller, so I want its captain to know I'm here. I shout a 'hello' at the open wheelhouse door. A man appears. He is surprised to see a swimmer in the water, while I'm equally surprised to see a man wearing a deerstalker and tailored Harris tweed suit. I tell him I'll be swimming around the back of his boat. I'm wearing earplugs and can't hear him, but I see his mouth move and there's a nod, which is good enough. As I swim across the bay I wonder what business the well-dressed captain has in this far-flung, sparsely populated corner of the country. He's obviously not a fisherman.

Walking back to the tent, post-swim, I see a group of people wearing military-style clothing board his vessel, which then heads out across the bay towards Taransay. They have serious looking equipment and I wonder if they could be army personnel on a training exercise.

Later I find out that the isle of Taransay and the nearby Borve Estate are owned by the same people. My hypothesis about them being military was incorrect, but they are armed. The well-dressed geezer works for the estate and is taking a group of paying guests across the bay to shoot stag.

I imagine the hunt on Taransay. The weapon is raised. The hunter centres the cross hairs and holds their breath as they squeeze the trigger. The animal has no idea it's chewing its last mouthful. The firing pin strikes the primer and ignites the propellant, which pressurises the cartridge, accelerating the bullet on its journey down the weapon's barrel, through air, then through flesh and onto its final destination, a beating heart. Which that little movement of an index finger will stop forever.

You may imagine that paying to end a large mammal's life would entail ownership of said creature, yet this is not so. The arrangement is merely target rental. Post-hunt, the corpse remains the property of the estate. Its executioner is however permitted to purchase body parts at market rates.

The hiring of live targets such as stag and grouse isn't a pastime for a people such as myself. It's far too expensive, and anyhow killing isn't something I want to make a hobby of. This is why I feel a fraud phoning the estate asking for prices and details of hunting on the island.

Life in the Hebrides is different to mainland Britain, with its own language, culture, history and pace of life. Talking to the press, the owners of Taransay appear keen to ingratiate themselves with the islanders, stressing their connection with Harris. That's understandable, as there's nothing Hebrideans love more than a good gossip. This is a tight-knit community where resentment against landlords is common because of the island's history of greedy, land-hogging gentry. A situation which eventually led to the Highland Clearances, when families were moved off their crofts, frequently into poverty, by greedy landlords to make way for sheep and deer grazing.

The owners of Taransay are privileged. They were brought up in New Zealand, Canada and the UK. The family own at least one other home in London, and they have a global outlook in their personal and business lives. Quoted in *The Scotsman*, they describe their feelings about the purchase of the island: 'It had to be right from a business sense . . . but it was mixed in with a big dollop of emotion as well.'

They say how they like to watch dusk fall behind the twin hills of Taransay from the Borve Estate. Given a certain mindset I can imagine it could be satisfying to look out at an island you own, from an estate on a nearby island you also own, in the knowledge that you can always go back to your London home whenever you like. Me, I'm thankful that for the price of swimming trunks and a pair of goggles I can be in the business of swimming. No island, second home or country estate necessary.

***

The backdrop for the ceremony is the white sand of Luskentyre Beach, and the view a few miles across the turquoise water of the bay towards our camp site. The coffin bearers slowly lead the procession across the windswept grass. The casket is set down near the open grave, then after a reading it is slowly lowered into the loam. This is what Rita and I witness when we stop the car to look at the map in a lonely spot overlooking Luskentyre Cemetery, quite likely the most beautiful place on Earth to be buried.

Though the coffin's occupant is unknown to us, as we look out of the car window and watch it descend out of sight, we both feel the dagger of sadness.

The cultural difference between the mainland and these islands is to be seen in this beautiful and romantic ceremony in which the deceased make their final journey, lowered into the ground by the muscle power of friends and family. For the majority of people in Britain that final passage will be made on a conveyor belt in a crematorium. For an industrial culture perhaps the mechanisation of this final ceremony is fitting.

London has two main ingredients, time and human energy. Their purpose: to make money. Unless there's wonga involved time isn't something to waste on a conversation. And who can blame anyone for that, because the place is run like a meter in one of the city's black cabs – no money, no ride. It's different in the Hebrides. Here conversation has a value of its own, which is perhaps what happens at a population density of nine people per square kilometre. Time slows, there is space, and mental calmness prevails, the taxi meter runs at an entirely different tempo. A chat with a stranger is unhurried, a source of interest and pleasure.

***

At a sheep auction near Portree on Skye, despite watching the tough ruddy faces closely I can identify only a few of the more obvious bidders. A raised eyebrow or the slightest glance at the babbling, hammer-wielding auctioneer is enough. These are farmers, yet the atmosphere is charged with the guarded emotions of hustlers at a poker table. Luckily I don't develop a facial tic; it might have resulted in the absurd spectacle of a Nissan Micra full of unwanted sheep. Outside the auction is a pen full of white sheep, and one black one, which reminds me of me.

Sheep and wool have long been an important part of the Hebridean economy. Harris' cottage industry of weaving woollen fabric has miraculously survived cheap labour and mechanised competition from overseas, thanks to a careful nurturing of the Harris tweed brand. The upshot is that islanders like Rebecca Hutton can still make a living weaving classy hardwearing fabric in their garden workshops.

We hear about Rebecca from the Harris tweed shop in Grosebay. As soon as I see their Italian tailored jackets I know where the Borve Estate's captain acquired his outfit. I try a jacket on and instantly look as though I could afford an island. Taking it off, I return to the ranks of peasantry. I don't buy one.

The beauty of the Hebridean coastline does nothing to shake the feeling of doom as I swim at other beaches. But it isn't the jellyfish, of which there are many. At least in part it's the remoteness and the cold. These islands are less tamed, more vital, and this makes me feel a mere speck in their magnificence. Of course there is risk when swimming off Brighton Beach, but I feel it more here. The fear reduces as soon as I enter the water, but I am unable to shake it off entirely.

Why do I let fear infest my psyche? After all, a life without risk is impossible, and to live without it would be dull, a form of living rigor mortis. But without a crystal ball how do we know which fears are phantoms of the night, and which we should listen to?

There is no recorded case of death by jellyfish in Britain. Regardless, most swimmers I know are scared of them. And what about the fear planted in the minds of my swimming friends by the film *Jaws*? It's completely out of proportion to the risk. Death or limb amputation by car crash is far more likely than a shark attack. I self-censor films involving sharks because I don't want my drama instinct triggered.

Humans are not good at calculating odds. Or, rather than anything so exacting as calculation, we have *feelings* about risk, which are often out of sync with the probability obtained from data. Our relationship with risk is not rational. That is perhaps why we sometimes need to ignore fear.

The comforts of modern living were late arriving in the Hebrides, with mains electricity connected only in the late 1950s. For around 200 years the population of Scotland's Highlands and Islands lived by crofting (small-scale agriculture on family plots of between two and five hectares). Fishing was, and still is, an important part of the economy. Risk was intrinsic to the hard manual labour of crofting and fishing in the harshest of climates, with little or no medical treatment available for the victims of illness or accidents. Today crofting has more or less vanished, though its cultural influence lives on.

It should come as no surprise that the British military were keen to recruit from the Western Isles, because of the

sheer toughness of a people used to grinding physical toil, who walked prodigious distances even in old age, who memorised complex genealogies, catechisms, poems and Scriptures, who slaughtered their own cattle, sheep and fowl, who washed and buried their own dead, who lived vigorously on a scant plain diet and had – amidst discomfort and griefs beyond our comprehension – the most enormous fun.

JOHN MACLEOD, *When I Heard the Bell*

Seven thousand Hebrideans fought in the First World War. For more than a thousand of them the Hun's marksmanship proved incurable. It is impossible to know the balance of death, how many Germans the Hebrideans killed.

Amidst the clanking sound of the human-powered loom, I watch the shuttle firing to and fro in Rebecca Hutton's garden shed, as she turns woollen yarn into classy looking Harris tweed. I get to thinking this is like life. We are the shuttle passing through the warp of existence, our experience woven into the fabric of our reality. For the people of Lewis there is a common thread in the fabric of their collective psyche, an event which is both wound and bond in their community.

BEASTS

If you are not willing to risk the unusual, you will have to settle for the ordinary.

JIM ROHN

On Hogmanay 1918, hundreds of tough, war-weary Hebridean servicemen were on their way home, arriving by troop train at the port and railhead at Kyle of Lochalsh. The Admiralty had messed up plans to get them home. The ferry which plied the seventy-mile route from the Kyle to Stornoway, the *Sheila*, was not large enough to carry all the men, and so another vessel, the steam yacht *Iolaire* (*Eagle* in Gaelic), was brought from Stornoway to carry the Lewis men home.

The atmosphere at the port was electric. There was laughter and joking, kitbags were stuffed with presents, the men were impatient to be reunited with their loved ones. With 280 souls including 24 crew aboard, the *Iolaire* pulled away from the pier and a great cheer went up. The weather was fair. Smoke belching from her funnel, the steam yacht headed north by west up the Inner Sound, steaming past the islands of Raasay and Rona and out into the Minch. Back home, relatives were baking and cleaning and making preparations for the men's arrival.

One of the men aboard the *Iolaire* was 27-year-old Kenneth Macphail from Arnol in north Lewis. A strong, stocky, good-looking man, no stranger to the precarious nature of life during war, he had an outstanding ability to survive. You could say he was a typical Hebridean, tough, capable and multi-skilled. Back home his family farmed a croft and owned a share in a fishing boat.

He lay on his back on the floor of the *Iolaire*'s crowded saloon, kitbag for a pillow. While the men around him were loud and excited, he was in a state of quiet reflection, thinking back over the things he'd witnessed during the war, Winston Churchill's ineffective naval bombardment of the Dardanelles and the disastrous landing of troops for the invasion of Gallipoli, when the turquoise water of the Aegean turned red with the blood of Allied soldiers. Yet it wasn't those events which haunted him. What did had occurred only fourteen months earlier, further west in the Mediterranean.

At midday on 31 October 1917, Commander Lothar von Arnauld de la Perière, captain of German U-boat 35, viewed the *Cambric*, a British merchant vessel, through his periscope. He was the deadliest submarine commander in history, not a man you wanted anywhere near your ship. While U-boat 35 paced the *Cambric*, von Arnauld coolly inspected the vessel through his periscope and noted it was armed. He decided to use a torpedo to sink his prey. After careful calculations and positioning, he gave the order, '*Torpedo los*,' and the weapon was set free. At the same moment he started his stopwatch. As the torpedo ran there was silence among the pungent submariners. Then they heard the thud of the explosion and through the periscope von Arnauld viewed his handiwork. He saw a man run to his post behind a gun on the burning ship's deck. That man was Kenneth Macphail from the Isle of Lewis.

***

Soon the *Cambric* is listing badly. It's going to sink. Macphail slides into the water and swims clear. A few moments later U-boat 35 surfaces, but on the opposite side of the stricken ship. Macphail therefore doesn't see it pick up four survivors. The sub dives and is gone. The *Cambric* sinks.

Back on the *Iolaire* Macphail's mind goes back to that lonely moment in the Mediterranean, when his ship is sunk and so far as he knows he is the only survivor. He tenses as he thinks about the risk of German submarines, then relaxes as he remembers the war is over and he's safe on a Royal Navy vessel heading for home. His thoughts drift again; he's alone in the water off the Algerian coast. Though he's a strong swimmer the drag of his clothing and the life vest slow progress. After some hours a search and rescue boat passes. He yells frantically but they don't spot him.

He is utterly demoralised, but he's a fighter and doesn't give up. He thinks of his family back in Lewis and continues swimming through the night. The water temperature is 22 °C and by morning his core temperature has dropped, but the rising sun offers warmth and comfort. He continues swimming south. By afternoon he's badly dehydrated, but the distant sight of land gives him the will to continue. At dusk he reaches the shallows and tries to stand, but his legs won't support him. Some locals spot a bedraggled figure on all fours at the water's edge. They run into the sea and drag him to safety. He is delirious but can sense these men are friendly. They remove his wet jacket and shirt. One of them puts his own jacket on Macphail. He's made landfall in a small Algerian village, where he is treated with kindness and taken to a nearby house. Later he is transferred to hospital, then given six months' leave for recuperation.

The *Iolaire* continues northwest into the dark. The mood aboard has changed as the men reflect on their wartime experiences and lost friends. A storm is brewing and rain lashes the windows, but it's warm and comfortable in the saloon. Not so for those on deck. Since his experience on the *Cambric*, Macphail has been haunted by the dagger of survivor's guilt. His crewmates from the *Cambric* won't be coming home. His thoughts are interrupted when an old friend from his home village leans over and gives him a friendly punch on the shoulder. They look at each other. The look of people who know each other well, the sort of look that says 'I understand'. They don't speak. These two men have escaped war physically unharmed but like most aboard, their souls are scarred for life.

The closer the *Iolaire* is to home, the stronger the yearning for loved ones. At the stroke of midnight in the middle of the Minch, as 1918 becomes 1919 the men sing 'Auld Lang Syne'. The singing continues with a couple of songs in Gaelic, but the mood is sombre, the singing lacks gusto and soon peters out. Yet there is hope, that vile war is over and all bodes well. Peace and tranquillity will surely follow the unspeakable events of the past four years.

After midnight the weather deteriorates. There are squalls accompanied by heavy rain showers. The Force 8 southerly gale over a long fetch has built a substantial following sea, making for a wallowing motion aboard. The army men feel seasick, while the sailors are unperturbed. The vessel is making good speed, about 10 knots. At 0100 the captain, Commander Mason, goes to his cabin leaving Lieutenant Cotter in command. Cotter and the coxswain are alone on the darkened bridge.

Strong currents, frequent gales, rapidly changing weather and the sheer number of obstacles make the Minch worthy of respect. Surprising then that the captain should return to his cabin for the most demanding part of the passage into Stornoway. The *Iolaire* is off course. It's travelled too far north. Some of its passengers are aware of this and are alarmed, yet the relationships of power mean that nothing is said. The vessel continues at full speed, cutting across the approaches into Stornoway harbour.

First contact with the Beasts causes the vessel to jolt and there is a scraping sound. Hearing this some of the men reach for their kitbags in the belief they are about to dock at Stornoway. But there is no mistaking the following impact. The scraping becomes a screaming as the iron hull grinds against ancient geology. It's not a fair contest. A featherweight against planetary material. The yacht's momentum takes her up onto the rocks known locally as the Beasts of Holm. The motion is violent. The mortally wounded vessel lists heavily, throwing many of the men on deck overboard.

Of all the nights to pick a fight with the Beasts, this is not it. The southerly wind combines with a strong current, turning the sea into a boiling cauldron of white foaming turbulence. Except there's nothing boiling about it; the sea temperature is just 8 °C.

Mauled by sea and rock, the hull is breached and distorting. Below deck, men in the saloon smash windows and climb through them. Most fall immediately into the seething water and are gone, some manage to clamber out and onto deck.

They are wrecked close to shore and only a mile and a half from Stornoway, but despite its proximity to the Hebridean capital this is a remote location. The *Budding Rose*, a fishing vessel, arrives on the scene but its crew cannot make an attempt at rescue because the *Iolaire* is trapped between the Beasts and land. Any attempt at rescue would be impossible in such conditions.

In the absence of assistance from land or sea, or from the officers on their own vessel, the men fend for themselves and each other. They launch two lifeboats. These are quickly swamped, and most of the men in them swept away.

Because of the low sea temperature, cold shock is inevitable upon immersion. Being smashed against the rocks by the sizeable sea is also probable. But despite the odds some make landfall, perhaps tossed ashore by a benevolent wave. Others make it onto the rocks, only to be returned to the sea by the deadly backwash pulling them, like the tentacles of a malevolent monster, across jagged rocks into the cauldron once more.

Those who have made it to shore yell across the thirty metres of spume for the men on the *Iolaire* to throw a line, but despite repeated efforts the rope falls short. It isn't only the temperature which causes men to freeze. Some are frozen by fear, unable to make the impossible decision: stay aboard as the vessel is mutilated or chance it in the hellish water. Both options are unfavourable.

John Macleod, a brave and generous-spirited man from Port of Ness, has made his decision. He knows which gamble he will take. As a man returning from war, the odds have favoured him so far. He strips to the lightest of clothing and throws his boots, which he will never recover, towards shore. He takes a slender heaving line and ties it to his wrist. This is risky, because the line could snag.

This is the swim of the century. Other swims, Olympic swims, recreational swims, record-breaking swims, are nothing in comparison. This is a swim that really matters. John Macleod has been watching the patterns in the waves. He chooses what he believes is the least terrible moment and leaps in, swimming like a maniac for shore. He's in the water perhaps for a minute. His strength, the waves and the gods favour him. The line he brings ashore is used to pull a heavier rope to land. Along this forty men pull themselves to safety.

On land men play a game of horizontal yoyo with the incoming waves and retreating backwash. Except it isn't a game. The incoming waves bring injured and dead men onto the rocks. The backwash pulls them back in. The game is to keep them on land.

The *Iolaire*'s boiler explodes. She breaks her back and sinks in the shallow water. Those left on board are done for, apart from one man who climbs the mast which is left protruding from the water.

The men who've made it to shore have to find shelter quickly, for without it they'll die of cold. There are no roads or paths and it's the darkest of nights. They have no shoes, their feet are cut and bruised, and many have been injured on the rocks. They make their way across ground covered with spiky gorse bushes. On a farm seven hundred metres away a slumbering family has no idea what apparition New Year's morning 1919 will bring.

***

Two hundred and one of those aboard died. None of the officers lived. Seventy-nine survived. The man who climbed the mast was rescued in the morning. He was the only person to arrive as all aboard should have, stepping ashore onto the quay in Stornoway.

It is said that in the days after the disaster, Kenneth Macphail's grief-stricken father Angus returned to the Beasts of Holm in a small boat, rowing to and fro trailing a grappling iron. After some days he hooked something heavy and pulled his son's corpse to the surface. In death Kenneth's hands were stuck fast in the pockets of his uniform. In a letter home written from hospital in Algeria some months earlier, Kenneth had told his family of the guilt he felt at being the only survivor of the *Cambric.* It is said his father believed his son had let himself die because of his grief. Sadly Kenneth never learned that four of his crewmates were picked up by U-boat 35 and survived the war. In the days following the disaster, carts piled high with bodies were driven through Stornoway, children orphaned, wives widowed, grief tearing at the heart of this close-knit island community.

To this day no one can be certain why the *Iolaire* struck the Beasts of Holm. On Lewis it is commonly believed the officers aboard the vessel were drunk. Certainly they were incompetent. It seems a fair bet that officers on land were drunk; it was after all New Year's Eve, which probably explains why no credible rescue attempt was organised from the naval base in Stornoway. The *Iolaire* had been overloaded and was not equipped with sufficient life jackets or lifeboats. This is perhaps yet another story of disaster by drunkenness and its close associate, incompetence.

The Admiralty held their inquiry into the disaster in private, not disclosing its findings until 1974. Most believe it was a whitewash. To add insult to injury, just six weeks after the disaster the Navy sold the *Iolaire*'s wreck to a salvage company still containing bodies.

The most competent seafarers aboard the *Iolaire* were its passengers, many of whom had worked as fishermen before the war, knew these waters well, and could have brought the vessel safely into Stornoway Town. To the British elite the Scottish islands were a source of manpower for their war machine. The attitude of that elite is summed up in the word they use for the men who give and receive the killing: infantry, the root of which is infant.

So far as I have been able to establish, there was only one conscientious objector to the First World War in the Hebrides. That man was Kenneth Macphail's brother. As the Chinese philosopher Lao Tzu says, *A man with outward courage dares to die; a man with inner courage dares to live.* The Macphail brothers had both kinds of courage.

The *Cambric* was one of 194 ships Commander von Arnauld sank during the Great War. Amidst the brutality of that conflict he had a very particular code of conduct, under which he strived to minimise loss of life. In doing so he would put his own vessel at risk by radioing a Mayday on behalf of the ships he sank, and in one case towing lifeboats back towards land:

I very rarely torpedoed a ship even when it was authorised. I much preferred the method of giving warning and doing my sinking by gunfire or by placing explosives aboard. In that way I saved torpedoes. And besides, I could accost the lifeboats, look over the ship's papers and get its name and tonnage.

VON ARNAULT, quoted in Lowell Thomas, *Raiders of the Deeps*

The reason von Arnauld sank Kenneth Macphail's ship with a torpedo without warning, killing twenty-four sailors, was precisely because it was armed. He couldn't afford to issue a warning for fear of being sunk himself. Had he done so it would have been Kenneth Macphail firing at his submarine rather than the other way round. Arming the *Cambric* had the opposite of the intended effect. Had it not been armed, its whole crew would most likely have been taken prisoner and all would have survived the war.

How do we make sense of risk when what seem to be sensible precautions can have the opposite of their intended effect? The difficulty is knowing what fears to listen to and which to ignore.

During my time in the Hebrides I meet fear and risk halfway and swim timidly close to shore. I have learned that risk and fear are not the same thing.

BUREAUCRAT

If you are going to sin, sin against God, not the bureaucracy. God will forgive you but the bureaucracy won't.

HYMAN RICKOVER

Back in Brighton, I hear from the swimmers that a small yacht has washed up on Brighton beach. Given my fascination with wrecks I run down to the beach to investigate. I find on the shingle a small 18-foot twin-keel sailing boat. Chatting to its distressed owner, a resourceful guy of about twenty, I learn that as a solution to a housing problem he had planned to live on this boat. First he'd got himself a mooring in his hometown of Folkstone, then he'd scoured the country looking for a boat.

This resourceful and intrepid guy found a suitable small yacht in Southampton and bought it for £200. Sailing back home from Southampton he got as far as Brighton when the rudder broke. He lost control of the vessel, which washed up on the beach. When the tide went out, his little boat was left high and dry on the shingle.

Coastguard operatives questioned him and searched the vessel but found nothing illegal. Next to give him grief were the council, who didn't want his boat on their beach. That afternoon he left the beach to attend to some personal business, telling the council workers he'd be back in an hour. On his return he found a rough-terrain forklift dragging what was left of his boat up the beach.

First the council workers had attached the towline to the mast, pulling it and a large chunk of the cabin roof off. They reattached their towline. This time the powerful machine tore away one of the boat's keels, rendering it a complete write-off. A kindly council bureaucrat assured its owner they would not charge him for removing the vessel. I was furious and advised the owner to seek compensation, but the guy had a gentle nature and seemed a lot less angry about it than me.

The sight of the stranded yacht reminds me of Jaywick, and the yacht left unmolested on its beach. Being ignored by the powers that be, as the whole of Jaywick is, clearly has advantages.

***

When one rows it is not the rowing which moves the ship: rowing is only a magical ceremony by means of which one compels a demon to move the ship.

FRIEDRICH NIETZSCHE

The point in moving to Brighton was to swim – and that means swimming all year round. When the sea temperature dropped to 8 °C I started wearing neoprene shorts, but I haven't bothered with gloves or boots. Strangely my hands seem to warm up quicker if I don't wear them. Other swimmers report the same, but post-swim, even in my fur-lined boots and two thick pairs of socks my feet take a couple of hours to warm up.

It's January and the sea temperature has dropped to 5 °C. A scientific explanation of cold-water swimming might incorporate neuroscience and factors such as endorphins, blood circulation and serotonin. But what is an endorphin? It's a name for something we can't really imagine. That's often a problem with scientific explanations, they aren't something we can relate to. So, as we live in the era of post-truth, where feelings are more important than facts, I'll try another explanation.

We all have our demons, and everyone knows demons like the heat of hell. Plunging yourself into the cold sea, it feels as though your skin is burning. This tricks your heat-seeking demons into believing you're on fire and, seeking heat, they rush to the surface of your skin. But when they get there, rather than heat they find intense cold. They hate cold and are quickly rendered catatonic. Because of this their tentacles, which they normally wrap around your psyche, retract into their ugly wart-encrusted little bodies.

As you continue swimming the little bastards are trapped near the surface of your skin where they get colder and colder, which makes them smaller and smaller until they almost disappear. If you stay in more than a couple of minutes your skin stops feeling as though it's on fire and just feels numb. By that time your demons are out for the count.

Because your personality is now demon free you become more human. You are friendlier, laugh more easily, are more relaxed, more intelligent, happier, kinder and more loving. This makes you more attractive and likeable. It's how people *think* they are when they're drunk or have taken cocaine. But unlike those drugs the effect is real. If you're lucky your demons will remain dormant for the rest of the day. Overnight they may well have recovered and be back in the business of dragging you down, but the good news is that demons have rubbish memories, so you can play this trick on them as often as you like.

It's midwinter and I've made the illogical switch from neoprene shorts back to normal trunks. It wasn't an easy transition. I did it because having less equipment simplifies things, and also because I experience more of the experience.

Dumping the neoprene, though, is the dumbest thing to have

done. Because it's arrived, the Beast from the East, a blast of cold Siberian air. The front pages of newspapers are covered with pictures of a snowy nation. Rarely does Brighton get so cold, well below freezing, and I've had my first experience of swimming in snow – which is quite unlike singing in the rain, although walking down the beach barefoot there is a wish to be light on one's feet as they make contact with the freezing white carpet.

In water at 4 °C, heat leaves a human body faster than a property developer passing a brown envelope to a planning official. Symptoms of a heart attack include a feeling of uselessness in one or both arms, and a sense of impending doom. There's no feeling of doom, which is how I know I'm not having one. Neither is there any gloom, in fact negativity has been blasted to kingdom come by sensations nothing short of mental and physical dynamite.

I no longer feel pain when entering the water, not even the ice-cream head. It's more a case of acute discomfort. I've either become desensitised or acclimatised, or maybe they amount to the same thing, like eating spicy food. If you eat it often enough the spiciness stops burning, yet you can still taste and enjoy it.

This is a mind-blowing way to start a day. Walkers on the prom stop to gawp at the dozen or so of us eccentric semi-naked loonies as we launch ourselves off the snow-covered beach into Mother Nature's refrigeration fluid. Post-swim, as large fluffy snowflakes float down, there's euphoric chatter and joking. This is most powerful and instantaneous antidepressant known to humanity.

A clinical study of the psychological effects of cold-water swimming would be worthwhile, but as it isn't a product, not a drug, there can be no profit. Without profit such a study cannot be funded, and without evidence to the contrary, they'll continue dishing out the happy pills, when maybe all that's needed is a swim.

The following day the air is still below freezing, while the sea temperature has dropped to 3.3 °C. The wind chill is brutal so we change in the lee of a breakwater, with the thin winter sun providing comfort and joy, but zero heat. This time it's a four-minute swim. That small drop in water temperature is noticeable and though the swim is two minutes shorter than yesterday's I feel just as cold afterwards. I have learned not to stay in too long, otherwise warming up takes hours and leaves me feeling sleepy. Today I experience the same psychic dynamite – although this is less like conventional explosives, and more like a nuclear deterrent to depression.

DEMOLITION

A few years ago the city council of Monza, Italy, barred pet owners from keeping goldfish in curved bowls . . . saying that it is cruel to keep a fish in a bowl with curved sides because, gazing out, the fish would have a distorted view of reality. But how do we know we have the true, undistorted picture of reality.

STEPHEN HAWKING

I have a foolproof cure for a hangover. It's so effective I'm surprised it isn't universally practised: it's called not drinking. I'm on day nine of it.

Yes, guilty as charged. I've kept on swimming through the dark Satanic winter, but as the writing faltered so the drinking gradually increased. I can't make out if it's because the drinking had been increasing that the writing foundered or because the writing was decreasing that the drinking was increasing. Whichever it was, the two are linked. I was starting to feel like a goldfish in a bowl, separated and out of touch with the world, seeing it through the distorted concave wall of my glass prism prison. I've made another promise to myself not to drink for a month.

One thing that hasn't faltered is the swimming, even though the air temperature has remained below zero and the water isn't far off freezing. Online I found a video of a wave freezing as it broke onto a beach in Kent. The week's rare combination of northeasterly storms, low sea temperature and low spring tides has caused the largest die-off of sea creatures in recorded history. Beaches on the east coast are ankle deep in the corpses of dead starfish, lobsters, little fish, crabs, mussels and other small invertebrates, and if I was in the sea longer than maybe fifteen minutes I'd be dead as well.

I meet Cecile at seven in the morning for an early swim. Sea temperature 3 °C, air -2 °C. We change in the lee of the stone breakwater near Marrocco's cafe in Hove, which gives some shelter from the vicious wind chill. Me, the nightly boozer, would not have got to the beach at this unholy hour. The clear-headed me has sprung out of bed keen for another dose of cold-water depression demolition.

Fear is along for the ride, but not to the extent it was in the Hebrides. I ignore it and again experience pins and needles in my hands, which after the first few minutes become completely numb, feeling only returning to them twenty minutes after I get dressed.

***

The human brain is a complex organ with the wonderful power of enabling man to find reasons for continuing to believe whatever it is that he wants to believe.

VOLTAIRE

It's day twenty-six of not drinking. The gravitational pull of the supermarket booze aisles has been less intense this time round. My strategy has been to steer clear of situations involving booze, which in our culture means all socialising. I miss it. But my resistance to drinking is bolstered by my new consciousness of my relationship with alcohol, an understanding of the destructive feedback loop it sucks me into as my mind becomes a washing machine of emotions laundered in the detergent of booze, tumbling round and round in a wash cycle of anxiety and depression.

Observing a friend who lost his dad to alcohol I'm concerned to see the potential for history to repeat with his own young boy. I gently enquire about his alcohol consumption. *Bullshit* is my unexpressed thought as he tells me his drinking isn't a problem because he once stopped for a week and could do so again. That's just the sort of thing I've said about my own drinking.

***

I failed my way to success.

THOMAS EDISON

I did it, another month of sobriety. It wasn't so difficult this time round and it's proof to self that I have at least some control. A bit like swimming is proof to self of the will to life.

MARTIAN

Total physical and mental inertia are highly agreeable, much more so than we allow ourselves to imagine. A beach not only permits such inertia but enforces it, thus neatly eliminating all problems of guilt. It is now the only place in our overly active world that does.

JOHN KENNETH GALBRAITH

Summer is back and I'm in the zone. There is a rhythmic splashing sound as I jog west through the inch-deep water covering the sand exposed by a low spring tide. The evening sun is 30 degrees above the Martian horizon and reflecting off the shallow water, its intensity reduced by sunglasses. As I pant the air feels warm entering and leaving my lungs.

I let my mind go where it wants, and it wants to be in the future on the surface of Mars. Humans have colonised the Red Planet and built utopia. It looks pretty cool. I pass a dad who's running around in the shallows, son on his shoulders, utter bliss on their faces. Kids doing cartwheels, couples playing beach ball, sandcastle building, dogs who have trained their owners to throw balls. The beach is busy with happy-looking people. 'Wow,' I think to myself, 'it turned out well building a colony on Mars.'

A beach is a landform alongside a body of water consisting of loose particles of rock, sand, gravel, shingle, or pebbles. The particles can also be of biological origin, such as mollusc shells or coralline algae.

Wikipedia

Quite a good definition, but there is so much more to a beach than its physical qualities. And I should know, because since beginning this book, I've spent lots of time on lots of beaches, and while on them I've been people watching. I jog on and my mind returns through the rubicon of daydreaming into the present. And I'm back on Earth, on Brighton Beach.

All people who come to the beach are idiots. So I was informed by a lifeguard in Hastings, who wrongly assumed the camaraderie of swimming would mean I'd share his sentiment. I've met policemen who share a similar way of thinking, and it's easy to see how, in such roles, this kind of mindset can develop. But the truth of it is, we are all idiots sometimes, and it can be a release to let one's hair down and be one.

Another truth is that the beach has a unique energy which has a liberating effect on the psyche. The beach is where even the businessman can un-suit and get busy with the far more important business of play, fun and relaxation. Perhaps it's this unshackling of the human spirit which can unnerve those of a more guarded and authoritarian disposition.

Where else but the beach is it acceptable to be semi-naked in public, or on some beaches completely naked? In what other public domain can we lie down, close our eyes and fall asleep? Where else are you free to rub oil onto your half-naked self and likewise your companion, to run and skip and dig and shout and laugh and fly a kite, to bury your friends and family in sand, to picnic, drink, and build sandcastles with equally happy children? The beach is the place that puts the sand in sandwiches and the free in freedom. Because it is free of charge, and your sandwiches will have that extra crunch.

It's a place where everyone is on public display and yet people are less inhibited. It shares this disinhibiting property with alcohol, except there's no hangover and no liver damage. Here, your car, your house and the other symbols of your position in the pecking order aren't visible, so you can let go of status anxiety as well.

But within this zone of psychic liberation there is etiquette. The selection of your temporary seaside territory involves careful clandestine observation and consideration. Walking out onto the sand or shingle you'll surreptitiously scan the beach personnel, measuring up your potential neighbours, maybe avoiding that rowdy group of beer-swilling lads with a boombox, choosing instead a friendly Sikh family munching their way through an extensive picnic of Indian cuisine. Density of population also comes into the equation. Your territorial claim mustn't be too close to others, and to be noticed staring at people's bodies would be poor form. To be in this seaside playground on a hot summer's day is to be a part of something. You can't help but absorb its energy, the smiles and joy are contagious.

As I jog onwards I have a sudden epiphany – we don't have to colonise another planet to build utopia, we already have it here on earth. It's called the beach. Being on the margins of land, able to see the horizon, to smell the sea, the reflexology of walking barefoot, the soporific sound of small summer waves breaking on the shoreline. Every sense is pleasantly stimulated, and in this domain you will not be insulted by walls, doors or fences. Sharing the openness with other beachgoers opens the human heart.

Even on a filthy rainy winter's day the beach retains the power to banish depression. That's the sort of time you can be completely alone in this empty expanse – you, the squawking gulls and the spindrift. This is when the fact you aren't sharing the beach means something. You are the only person idiot enough to be there, and that feels good. The sort of day you have to do the reverse of breathing, when you open your mouth and struggle to prevent your lungs becoming a pair of over-inflated balloons. The planet wants to impress you with her huge waves ploughing into the shoreline.

Jogging onwards, suddenly the mood changes. The beach is empty. The spell is broken. If I needed evidence this would surely be it, that more is truly less. There's no line in the sand; instead there's a sign further up the shingle which says *Private Beach.* I've arrived at a bunch of seafront houses known locally as Millionaires' Row. Aren't the rich supposed to have more fun? Well, it sure doesn't look like it. I ignore the sign and continue west.

***

It's pretty hard to tell what does bring happiness; poverty and wealth have both failed.

KIN HUBBARD

A few days after my return from the Red Planet I'm swimming alone, eastwards from Portslade towards Hove. It's another beautiful sunny day in early summer. I'm a hundred metres from shore, directly opposite Millionaires' Row. Travelling in the opposite direction is a young guy paddling a sit-on-top kayak. As our paths cross he capsizes. I stop. Every time he tries to get back on, he falls off on the opposite side. I swim over and attempt to steady his craft for him. This time he falls out on top of me, pushing me underwater. When I surface I see panic in his eyes. I figure the best course of action is to get him to land. 'Let me help you get the kayak back to shore,' I say.

I hold onto the front of the kayak and do breaststroke legs backwards. He clings onto the side, kicking his legs. He's still looking uncomfortable. I notice a family on Millionaire's Beach. We are going to make landfall close to them. I'm hoping they'll help us out of the water, but they studiously ignore us. An inner voice says, 'All people who own private beaches are idiots.' This is answered by the voice of reason which tells me, 'stop being a prick, you're thinking like that lifeguard in Hastings.' And the truth of it is that I could have done a lot better myself. I should have given the kayaker some advice – *wear a buoyancy aid*. But I say nothing and leave him paddling unsteadily away.

BOURGEOIS

Success consists of going from failure to failure without loss of enthusiasm.

WINSTON CHURCHILL

What's the point in being a writer who can't think? My grey matter has again become grey, when what a writer needs is technicolor. The reason for the monochrome mind is too much booze. So I decide to stop drinking for another month. But after just two weeks: failure. I've started drinking again. I'm deciding not to let this failure drag me down into despair. But it's serious. Unless I substantially reduce the drinking or stop altogether I'll most likely be going to an early grave.

***

The best way to deal with procrastination is to postpone it.

TONY ROBBINS

Remember address books? I found a decades-old one on my bookshelf. Flicking through its torn tatty pages, bearing doodles absentmindedly penned during long-forgotten phone calls, I was struck by the number of entries, friends from my past, there'd be absolutely no point in trying to rekindle a connection with – owing to them being dead.

I've started seeing dead people. I see them in the street and think 'Oh, there's so and so'. Until the realisation comes crashing in . . . They're dead.

Tick tock, the hands of the undertaker's clock turn, relentlessly slicing away the future, rendering the repudiation of death unviable and procrastination ridiculous.

***

A lot of the changes are so gradual that they don't even qualify as news, or even as interesting: they're so mundane that we just take them for granted. But history shows that it's the mundane changes that are more important than the dramatic 'newsworthy' events.

ROBERT D. KAPLAN

The signs are everywhere. This morning I cycled down a small cut-through off some random urban backstreet. At the beginning of it a respectable-looking middle-aged woman stood waiting. As I continued down the cut-through I was met by a procession of zombies. Or perhaps they were moths. Walking the walk of the dead they came towards me, an absurdly thin woman with a black eye, a tall sad-looking man with sunken cheeks, followed by a skeleton on legs, his bony cranium covered by an uneven crewcut. Others, maybe seven of them, had suffering and ill-health etched deep into their faces.

Where had they come from, and where were they going? The penny dropped as I looked over my shoulder and saw them gathered around the respectable-looking woman. Her image, like a purveyor of alcohol, was a sham. A candle to the zombie moths, she was handing over small packages, bomblets of temporary psychic escape. I wondered how such tragedy had touched this terminal procession of addicts. The answer is almost certainly, *gradually*.

Gradually is a kind of disguise, until its camouflage suddenly falls away and it jumps out of a bush shouting 'Fooled you!' I can now see this has been the case with my decades-long drift into alcohol addiction.

Suddenly I realise that *gradually* is something to look out for in all areas of life. One gradual shift that concerns me, not a personal one, but on the macro scale, is the gradual drift into the surveillance state in which all our personal communications and behaviours are monitored. Introduced suddenly, this would have been shocking and unacceptable. Introduced gradually, most people have accepted it. It's all very well while the state is benign, but when it turns there will be no way of stopping it. The prison camps will be full – of people like me.

But gradually isn't always bad. We can *gradually* make things better. *Gradually* is both friend and foe.

***

Rituals are important.

JOHN LENNON

I didn't realise why my friend Tam wanted to visit me in Brighton until she was struggling to get into a sea too rough and too cold for her swimming ability. It was then she told me it was the anniversary of her dad's death. His ashes had been scattered in the sea off the coast of her childhood home of Cape Town.

Getting in the sea on this date brings her closer to him, and even though it was too rough for her to swim, getting her legs in and being near the sea gave her comfort. This is a kind of magic. A ritual. A bringing together of living and dead.

***

Life begins at the end of your comfort zone.

NEALE DONALD WALSCH

Épater le bourgeois is French for *to shock the comfortable middle-class citizens.* To do so was the aim of much avant-garde art. There is something of *épater le bourgeois* in cold-water swimming. By doing so you shock your comfortable self out of the mundane limits of everyday life. You cannot deny your vulnerability in such a situation.

It seems as though the quantity and severity of depression is increasing in proportion to the increasing level of material comfort we have in society. Sea swimming is the opposite of comfort, which is perhaps why it has the opposite effect of depression. Because it challenges your inner bourgeois. Just a theory.

***

It is a part of probability that many improbable things will happen.
ARISTOTLE

I am one of a load of teenagers at a beach party. We have made a fire from driftwood. There is a view across Southampton Water to Fawley Oil Refinery, which in the dark looks like a futuristic city with flaming flare stacks and thousands of twinkling lights. Everybody is drunk and having fun. Suddenly I have what seems like a really good idea. I'll go and see my girlfriend. I walk a mile or so back to my motorbike, jump on it and head for her place. Halfway there I suddenly find everything has slowed down. Time has gone into a different dimension and I'm airborne. As I fly through the night air I think to myself, 'I went round that corner too fast.' My inflight thoughts are relaxed and unhurried. 'I'm about to die.' No fear, just that certainty. The next thing I know I'm in the afterlife. There's no sense of surprise; instead there is curiosity and it seems natural that thinking occurs after death – thoughts such as 'oh, so this is what it's like be dead' and 'it doesn't feel too bad to be dead' and 'in fact it's quite OK to be dead'. I take in my surroundings – quite dark and grassy. 'Funny there's grass in the afterlife.'

At first there was a tiny seed. Time was playing tricks. I couldn't say how long it took, but the seed gradually grew into a doubt. Was this really death? I was in a state of existential confusion. How could I possibly tell if this was life or death? I took a more detailed look at my surroundings and realised I was in a ditch. But this information didn't provide an answer to the question I unhurriedly pondered: 'How can I find out if this is life or death?'

An idea popped into my head. 'I should look beyond the ditch.' I stuck my head up, and there was my motorbike on its side in the road. Stopped cars and confused people walking about looking for the rider. This was definitely an earthly scene, and it convinced me I was alive, and remarkably uninjured.

Much to the surprise of the onlookers I jumped up out of the ditch, picked up the bent machine, restarted it and continued my journey.

Another lucky escape. The thing which surprised me about this odd experience was that at no point did I feel fear. Nor did I feel any particular elation at discovering I was still alive. I cannot say exactly why I recount this story. All I can say is that revisiting this strange experience is part of my investigation into what it means to be alive and therefore confronted with the certainty of death. I'm thankful fortune favoured the particularly dumb teenager I was, and that I didn't kill or injure anyone else.

***

We shall never know all the good a smile can do.

MOTHER TERESA

Looking unnervingly real and like they might jump, eighty-four life-size statues have been placed around the edge of two high-rise buildings in London. The art installation is a collaboration between suicide prevention charity Campaign Against Living Miserably (CALM) and artists Mark Jenkins and Sandra Fernandez.

The statues represent the eighty-four men who kill themselves during the average week in Britain (though I don't understand why they haven't included the ten women who also kill themselves). CALM's website gives the names of men who've killed themselves along with heart-wrenching testimonials as to their character. Unsurprisingly, it's the sensitive souls who end up self-destructing.

The installation makes me think of a man who committed suicide by hanging himself from a tree near one of my mooring spots on the River Lea. At that time I was working as a photographer and always carried a camera with me. I couldn't decide if I should photograph him or not. Eventually I did: I didn't want him to be forgotten. It's a haunting image. I wondered about his life and who he might have left behind. I am also reminded of Aaron from our boating community, who hanged himself from a tree near his boat.

***

Sensitivity is transmuted into suffering and disorders only when the world is unable to heed the exquisitely tuned physiological and psychic responses of the sensitive individual.

GABOR MATE, from *Scattered Minds*

In his book on attention deficit disorder, *Scattered Minds*, which I am reading to learn more about my own ADHD, Gabor Maté uses the following metaphor for the difficulties in maintaining a healthy mind in a less than healthy culture:

> On the westernmost shores of Canada, on Vancouver Island, one sees scruffy and twisted little conifers, stunted relatives of the magnificent fir trees that dominate the landscape just a short distance inland. We would be wrong to see these hardy little survivors as having some sort of plant disease: they have developed to the maximum that the relatively harsh conditions of climate and soil allow. If we wish to understand why they differ so dramatically from their inland relatives, we need to know under what conditions majestically tall, stout and ramrod-straight fir trees are able to thrive. It is the same with human beings.

Oh yes it is, and the damage is so widespread I wonder how many ramrod-straight humans there are left on the planet. Certainly not me.

There is something rotten going on in the state of human affairs if so many people want to kill themselves and so many others are depressed, or suffer from diagnosable psychiatric 'disorders'. It is wrong to use the term disorder to describe a healthy response to an unhealthy society. The term is not only misleading, it's a reversal of reality. Used in this way, the term disorder piles on even more pressure, implying that the person with the disorder is simply not sufficiently resilient.

The BBC *Horizon* programme 'Stopping Male Suicide' examines and offers advice on how suicide might be prevented. The documentary makers do what our politicians do, they completely ignore the impact of a sick society on mental health.

Trying to piece together the scattered jigsaw of life and death, I chat to Pete, a Coastguard worker who for twenty years has been recovering bodies from a suicide hotspot. I'm hoping to learn something from his experiences. He's asked me not to mention the location of his work because media coverage precipitates more suicides, a phenomenon known as suicide contagion.

Over his time in the role Pete has seen an increase from around ten to forty suicides a year. Some he manages to talk down. Some have jumped by the time he gets there. Others jump while he's talking to them. Some will jump unseen and unreported. Of the unseen jumpers, some of their bodies will never be recovered; no one will ever know what happened to them. This is particularly sad as the victims' loved ones are left in an everlasting state of uncertainty.

I ask how his job affects him emotionally, but he's reluctant to talk about it. I sense he's been touched deeply by his experiences and has his own private way of dealing with them.

I imagine what it must be like to test the laws of irreversibility. To pass the point of no return. To leap into the nonexistent arms of freefall. What does a person think *in extremis*? Surprisingly it is possible to get an idea from an article in the *New Yorker* titled 'Jumpers' by Tad Friend, who documented case studies of suicides from the Golden Gate Bridge, including the accounts of some of the very few survivors.

> Ken Baldwin and Kevin Hines both say they hurdled over the railing, afraid that if they stood on the chord they might lose their courage. Baldwin was twenty-eight and severely depressed on the August day in 1985 when he told his wife not to expect him home till late. 'I wanted to disappear,' he said. 'So the Golden Gate was the spot. I'd heard that the water just sweeps you under.' On the bridge, Baldwin counted to ten and stayed frozen. He counted to ten again, then vaulted over. 'I still see my hands coming off the railing,' he said. As he crossed the chord in flight, Baldwin recalls, 'I instantly realized that everything in my life that I'd thought was unfixable was totally fixable – except for having just jumped.'

> Kevin Hines was eighteen when he took a municipal bus to the bridge one day in September, 2000. After treating himself to a last meal of Starbursts and Skittles, he paced back and forth and sobbed on the bridge walkway for half an hour. No one asked him what was wrong. A beautiful German tourist approached, handed him her camera, and asked him to take her picture, which he did. 'I was like, "Fuck this, nobody cares," he told me. 'So I jumped.' But after he crossed the chord, he recalls, 'My first thought was What the hell did I just do? I don't want to die.'

Another case study from the article brought me to tears. On this occasion suicide was achieved. A note later found at the man's home read, 'I'm going to walk to the bridge. If one person smiles at me on the way, I will not jump.'

Mother Teresa was right about smiles, and she wasn't referring to the salesman's smile, but rather to smiles fuelled by love. Yet it seems we are creating a society with a genuine smile deficit, to the extent that for some self-destruction seems the only way out. Meanwhile others, including myself, struggle to maintain mental equilibrium, and many, including myself, are self-medicating with drugs and alcohol.

***

Why I want to go to this unmentionable place in Britain where so many people have thrown themselves into oblivion I can't say. All I know is that I want to know more about life, death and depression. In the car on the way there my friend Chris and I get into a stupid circular argument which hasn't been resolved by the time we arrive. I'm feeling stressed and uncomfortable in his company, and he probably feels the same. I don't tell him why I want to visit this place.

On arrival we walk along the cliff tops. Chris is taking selfies and standing too close to the cliff edge. While he's doing so a tough, agitated-looking guy comes within a few feet of us. I don't get a good vibe from him. I get the feeling he's mentally unstable and unpredictable. I have the sense he could push us over the edge, so I feel relieved when he walks off. Chris is in his own world and doesn't notice the guy. I watch him from a safe distance. I suddenly realise that maybe he isn't thinking about pushing someone off, but rather about throwing himself off.

I think about approaching him and asking if he's OK, but my concern for his wellbeing is overwhelmed by my sense of self-preservation. I watch in horror as he walks determinedly towards the edge, veering off at the last moment, walking parallel with the cliff top. I'm at a loss as to what to do.

Chris and I walk inland and back towards the car. When we reach it there are a handful of policemen nearby. Soon more cops arrive on foot, with the guy I thought might jump.

Thinking of the note left by one of the Golden Gate's Jumpers, I realise at the very least I could have smiled at him. I feel ashamed I did nothing to help.

***

The world is your lobster.

GEORGE COLE

A month or so after the situation on the cliffs, I'm enjoying the afternoon sun on my balcony while indulging in a spot of people watching. Across the street, a well-dressed man and woman are getting into a shiny open-top sports car. A punky-looking guy carrying a skateboard walks down the road. He's scruffy and could be homeless. Everything about him, including his overexuberant walk, says too many drugs, which I am about to find out have produced a sense of non-aggressive truthfulness. He sees the couple in the sports car and shouts across to them, 'That car's rubbish, I've got a skateboard.'

I giggle as sports-car couple try to pretend this isn't happening. The guy didn't buy his expensive shirt, classy haircut and flashy car so this kind of scenario could occur. This wasn't in the sales brochure. He and his good-looking female friend look sheepish. The facade of their tenuous image is showing signs of fragmentation. They lack the confidence to laugh at the situation. They drive off a little bit too hurriedly with their coolness blown to smithereens, leaving me laughing at the ridiculousness of human life on Earth. The smile is whipped off my face as I realise that within this comedy a tragedy is being played out. A tenuous sense of self is not funny at all, as I know only too well.

***

It's another summer's evening and I'm jogging along Brighton prom minding my own business when I see a little girl dancing with a unicorn to a man dressed in black playing the clarinet. 'Strange,' I think, 'why is no one else is noticing this beautiful scene?' Even the clarinet player appears oblivious. I stop and and watch. The girl is perhaps five, wearing little white socks. Her parents are probably on the beach, unaware of their daughter's antics. The unicorn is of course much bigger than her. She can hardly get her arms round the mythical creature, so the dance is awkward. But she's having a ball. She looks very very happy. The unicorn is under-inflated, but this doesn't spoil her fun. I jog on feeling uplifted by this magical spectacle. Beauty and comedy surround us and it's important to notice it. This summer on Brighton Beach there's been an outbreak of inflatable unicorns.

Inflatable lobsters are also on the increase. I watch with amusement as a sunburnt beach-going dad huffs and puffs inflating one for his impatient four year old. The tabloid headline . . . *Lobster Inflates Lobster.*

***

Piglet noticed that even though he had a Very Small Heart, it could hold a rather large amount of Gratitude.

A. A. MILNE

Bang. A set of canine teeth are inflicting puncture wounds on my mental flesh. So much for the summer bliss and watching the comedy of human life. To relieve the pain I so want to drink. How easy it would be to go to the supermarket for a bottle of Bulgarian Pinot Noir – or two. Instead I go to bed early, rising twelve hours later. When I do the quadruped's teeth are still embedded in my psyche.

The following evening it's even worse and the gravity of the booze aisle drags me into its orbit. I drink one bottle of wine. The next morning I feel low, but strangely not angry with myself.

Though I'm drinking again, my immediate mental state has improved. Thank god for swimming. A while ago I heard a guy on the radio talking about the benefits of keeping a gratitude log, so I've started keeping one. Here's mine from this morning . . .

> Woke in a comfortable bed after a peaceful night's sleep. I have a roof over my head and live in a nation which isn't engaged in war (at least not on its home turf).
>
> I walk downstairs experiencing no pain. All my limbs function (after having had arthritis this isn't something I take for granted). Breakfast of muesli, blueberries, fresh pineapple, kiwi fruit, topped off with a few spoonfuls of organic yogurt, washed down with Chinese loose leaf green tea, followed by a small but strong coffee, which I drink while

looking up today's weather and tides in preparation for today's swim. Bliss.

I'm grateful for the ease of life on land because living on the boat was hard work. The water tank had to be refilled every fortnight, which involved moving to a water source. Gas bottles for cooking had to be changed periodically, the toilet had to be emptied every couple of weeks, and logs for the wood-stove had to be cut, split, seasoned and stored. Small acts such as turning on a light, going to the toilet, turning on a tap all had a back story which involved management and work. This off-grid life was labour intensive. Living on-grid is so comfortable and so easy by comparison. I feel a sense of gratitude every time I turn on a tap, flush the loo or switch on a light.

***

It's been a month since the latest dog attack and it was short lived. This is evidence that things may be *gradually* changing for the better. And I am grateful for this too.

FOSSIL

As we peer back through the fossil record, through layer upon layer of long-extinct species, many of which thrived far longer than the human species is ever likely to do, we are reminded of our mortality as a species.

RICHARD E. LEAKEY

I'm off on another mini adventure, this time to Chapman's Pool on Dorset's Jurassic Coast. It shouldn't really be called a pool, and neither should this fossil-rich shoreline be called Jurassic; someone got the geological time period wrong. But the name sounds good and pulls in the grockles, of which I'm one.

Chapman's Pool is blessed by being a couple of miles from the nearest road, which even then is only a small country lane on which I don't see a single car. I set off on foot across gently undulating land of freshly cut stubble, while swallows show off their acrobatic skill dog-fighting invisible prey.

As that nemesis of the gluten intolerant comes into sight I understood where the peace-shattering mechanical noise is coming from: a combine harvester carving swaths through long ears of wheat, disgorging its booty into a trailer towed by a tractor. The scene is shrouded in dust and I can see why in the early days of mechanised farming, before air-conditioned cabs, combine drivers suffered from farmer's lung. To the ancestors, who would have done the same job by hand, a combine harvester would appear dragon-like with its roaring diesel engine, a dust cloud for smoke, and vomiting wheat in place of fire. I wonder how many people with scythes these mechanical dragons have replaced?

Reaching the edge of the valley I have an oblique view over the Dorset coast and Chapman's Pool itself, which would be better referred to as a cove. In centuries past the place was favoured by smugglers, and with Brexit perhaps it will be again. It's late evening, too late to be swimming alone, yet there is no doubt in my mind that I will, because not having done so for more than twenty-four hours there is a dangerous dog lurking in my metal hinterland.

The path down into the valley has been worn to bare soil by the feet of daytime fossil hunters, the last of whom must have left a couple of hours since. The pull of gravity is only slightly less than the grip of my sandals. At its steepest point some kindly person has left a rope, from which I get a practical demonstration of the laws of physics as friction turns to heat in my hands.

After a descent of one hundred metres I scramble down onto the beach. The shoreline is littered with boulders and loose material which has fallen from the cliffs. I look west, then east, considering which way to walk. The cliffs to the west are high. To the east they are lower and there is an uninhabited boathouse. There's not a soul in sight.

West or east? I ask myself. In my mind's eye I see myself walking west along the beach under those high cliffs. I'm looking down, fossil spotting, I see many, but they are embedded in rocks too heavy to carry home. Above I hear a dull thudding sound. I look up. There's no time to be terrified. I see a thousand tons of cliff accelerating downwards towards me. I also accelerate, into a run, but I have barely moved a couple of metres before it's upon me. The next thing I know I'm floating upwards, looking down at the pile of rock and mud beneath which my body is buried. There I lie dead under the fossil-rich debris, at the beginning of becoming a fossil myself.

I could have been a narwhal or a gnat, Planet Earth's incomprehensible impartiality is recording my existence in its own way. I don't rot. I'm dried and compressed, fused into sediment, imprinted into solid matter in much the same way I am when swimming in water, except in rock my legacy is visible for longer.

By 2042, after a protracted crisis, humans are extinct. Fast forward fifty million years and another species is dominant on the planet. They have a culture not dissimilar to our own, except they have a more harmonious society, and have four legs. They are a bit like dogs but their front legs are like human arms. Lets call them *Homo caninious*.

In the late Anthropocene human neuroscientists hadn't understood that the mental processing power required to balance our fundamentally unstable upright bipedal form overwrote a small social centre in our hippocampus, making it difficult for us to live cooperatively. The more balanced quadruped suffers no such deficiency, and consequently *Homo caninious* have produced a happy and harmonious society. No wars, depression or inequality.

Like us they have an interest in archaeology and prehistory. They find the fossil and archaeological record fascinating yet confusing. It's difficult to piece together what *Homo sapiens* were about, and why they suddenly became extinct. Exactly like humans, their view of history is blocked by their own mode of thinking. They cannot imagine a culture which would practise such a damaging form of economic exchange that it would cause a climate catastrophe and its associated conflicts which would finish us off.

Many millennia after the cliff fall which killed me, a *Homo ca-*

ninious named Zzjgizgh is on a fossil-hunting holiday and has spent the day happily picking through rocks and digging. She uses a trowel to dig and a hammer to break the rocks. Concentration creases her furry brow as she scrapes away loose soil to expose what looks like the elbow joint of a large mammal. She has found me.

A complete *Homo sapiens* – it's a rare find, which attracts international media attention. Zzjgizgh and the fossil, that's me, become famous. I'm given a name which is completely unpronounceable in human language. It sounds something like *Abcde*, which means Water Man.

My fossil shows that the individual was carrying something on his back. It's a rucksack, and what's inside it causes international speculation. Why was this *Homo sapiens* carrying goggles? Had *Homo sapiens* been making the transition back to water? Evolutionary scientists come up with all sorts of theories to explain it. They don't realise that fifty million years ago this geezer (me) just liked to swim.

In real life, of course I don't walk west under those high crumbling cliffs. Instead I head east. Here, even though the cliffs are lower, it's a reasonable precaution to walk as far away from them as possible, so I boulder hop along the water's edge heading for the boathouse on the far side of the cove. Outside it there's a slipway which should allow easy access to the water.

The mood has changed since strolling through the fields of stubble above. This is beginning to feel like a scene from a noir movie. A sense of impending dread is gnawing away inside my chest.

Since the doom-filled Hebridean swims I've learned more about this foe called fear, and how to deal with it. Rationality. I watch the sea and imagine the bay in plan view, and from this perspective I'm thinking it unlikely there will be currents capable of pulling me out to sea. I check the map and see that if I got into trouble I'd be able to swim a few miles east or west down the coast to a settlement – if I really had to.

Meanwhile I'm on the lookout for people. No one. The place is utterly deserted. I look up above the cliffs to the coast path. No one there either. I get undressed and pull my trunks on. The wind is picking up, the place feels desolate and unwelcoming. Loneliness, an almost constant companion in my life, blends horribly with fear. I know these feelings well. It's maybe five hundred metres to the other side of the cove.

The heatwave is over but the air and sea are still warm. I get in and let the water hold me. I swim. My view is of seaweed, over which I fly like a bird soaring above a forest canopy. Except I don't see this as beautiful. The weed spooks me. There could obviously be monsters hiding in it. I don't like it when it touches my body. I know I can't let these emotions spiral. That could lead to panic, and panic in water can lead to death. I make a conscious effort to remain calm. The seabed doesn't slope steeply and I'm fifty metres from shore before there is deep, weed-free water.

Well, it's my choice to be in the water, and here I am. Visibility is about two metres, large, widely spaced, fast-moving waves are barrelling into the cove from the open sea, stirring up sediment. The place feels ancient. I'm swimming in fossil ectoplasm, I'm a flea on the back of a huge creature called Planet Earth.

I have the feeling a large sea creature with senses I can't even imagine is watching me through the murk. Paranoia. 'Stay calm.' I swim across the bay, but stop before I reach the other side and tread water, rising and falling on waves which will soon commit mindless suicide against the margins of land. My legs feel vulnerable hanging down into the unknown. It's a long time since I've been this spooked, and it's spiralling. I need to break the spell.

For most people, the idea of dying alone is different to dying in company. This is primal. I am not ready to die either alone or in company. But I am alone, and I can feel death on my shoulder. I've underestimated my reaction to this barren place. This fear is irrational, but it's strong and I'm finding it difficult to control. I'm like a little boy on my own in a dark forest seeing faces in trees. Perhaps it's the psychic energy of billions of years of life and death etched into the cove's geology.

As I did when I entered the cove on foot, I look west then east. Only this time my eyes are just above sea level. This time I don't let my mind wander onto what might happen if I head west. I look back towards the boathouse. I need to be back on land. I swim east towards the slipway, dreading swimming through the weed again, but when I do I'm surprised to find myself unperturbed.

When things are going badly and people are frightened, that's when the mechanism of *épater le bourgeois* kicks in. Fear is a leveller. I walk back up the slipway and onto dry land. I'm humbled. Strangely I feel like crying, but I bottle it up.

That night I go to the local pub, the Square and Compass, which has views over the English Channel. The place is built out of chunks of Planet Earth, aka Portland stone. In a room finished in the unpainted rock, with oak panelling halfway up the walls, a folk band is playing to an appreciative audience. I stand absorbing an atmosphere of authenticity, listening to the music and observing the audience. Perhaps it's the result of my swim in fossil juice, but I'm swamped by the realisation that no one in this room will exist in seventy or so years. But this shared commonality doesn't scare me. I feel a sense of love for everyone present. What wonders that frightening swim worked.

***

Life comes at us in waves. We can't predict or control those waves, but we can learn to surf.

DAN MILLMAN

Who wins in a fight: waves or rock? The correct answer is waves. Though the process may take eons, they erode not only rock but whole landmasses, and through deposition they create them as well. Britain was once joined to France by a land bridge which was demolished by the mother of all tsunamis.

Before anyone had the idea of national anthems for Denmark, France or Britain, you could walk on dry land between these places. Fishing boats in the North Sea have dredged up archaeological artefacts which show that these waters were once dry land, and fertile hunting grounds for our ancestors. As the ice age receded, the sea rose and the waves moved in.

Waves have rhythm; they are part of the percussion section of orchestra Earth. Swimming also has rhythm. When swimming in a choppy sea I try to synchronise my rhythm with that of the ocean. But often that's impossible, because on steep or vertical shorelines, waves bounce back seawards, meeting and passing through incoming waves, creating a chaotic lumpy sea state, like friends at a rave who've had too many drugs and end up falling over each other. In that sort of sea your job is to keep your own rhythm within the discordant surroundings. It's a bit like a working in a job where you feel no connection with your colleagues, your boss or the work. You just have to get on with it and do your best to survive.

If you look closely you'll see that there are waves hitching a ride on the back of waves. I can see at least three layers of them, but I reckon there are more. Some of the biggest waves are sixteen-metre monsters which come regular as clockwork, every 12 hours 25 minutes. They are called tides.

It's impossible not to be awestruck by the power of gigantic storm waves waging their war of attrition against a rocky shoreline. And at the opposite end of the scale there's also an emotional reaction to those small lazy waves that caress a shoreline making soothing water-music, the anti-venom to the sirens and stress-inducing mechanical soundscape of the urban environment.

Strange are those waves that fill the space we live in. The space that isn't sea, but also isn't solid matter. The space containing the air we breathe is a maelstrom of waves. Mobile phones, Bluetooth, media broadcasts, GPS and satellite communications fill the ether with an invisible cacophony of electromagnetic radiation.

London and other cities in Britain have seen waves of German bombers. When I worked as crew on a gravel dredger in the Solent, we used to find evidence of the Luftwaffe's handiwork among our cargo in the form of unexploded bombs which we unknowingly hoovered up from the seabed. I began to wonder if some German aircrew had deliberately dropped their bombs off target because they felt waves of guilt for attacking civilian populations. But no matter, waves of Allied bombers would be going in the opposite direction a few years later to rain down firestorms and death upon German and Japanese cities.

As well as military action coming in waves, so do emotions – both within ourselves and between us and others. Like waves in the sea, these waves of collective consciousness bounce back off the step surfaces of human relations and pile up into confusing masses. When I first started cycling through the metropolis I began to think I could detect these waves. Some days I'd witness widespread anger and unhappiness, others I'd see good humour and smiles.

Cruelty creates waves of emotion which behave like the waves kicked up by an ocean storm, continuing long after the storm itself is over.

Waves of collective consciousness surround us. They are at different frequencies and amplitudes and travel in different directions. Some of these waves are small, affecting just a handful of people; occasionally there are monster waves, tsunamis of emotion which crash into the shoreline of humanity with devastating results.

Edward Munch's *The Scream* captures the transferable nature of human emotional energy. In it you can feel the protagonist's psychic pain which infests the fabric of the image. You can sense the will of passers-by on the bridge as they try unsuccessfully to keep the screamer's pain out of their own consciousness. It could easily be a scene from the Golden Gate Bridge.

The tangible signs of waves of collective psychic energy can take many forms. Often preceding large-scale conflict there will be a weaponisation of history, a conscious distortion and manipulation of popular sentiment by an elite using the media as its vehicle. This is done with the aim of whipping up collective waves of hatred. The out-group is described as less than human. Hatchets that have been buried are dug up. History is full of such examples. Waves of irrationality and hatred need to be neutralised as quickly as possible by waves of calm, positivity and goodwill, like those friendly hand waves between people when they are separated by a small space but wish to acknowledge each other. Those small acts of friendly recognition are a thing of beauty.

Everyone has the power to make waves.

***

O thou invisible spirit of wine, if thou has no name to be known by, let us call thee devil . . . O God, that men should put an enemy in their mouths to steal away their brains! that we should, with joy, pleasance revel and applause, transform ourselves into beasts!

WILLIAM SHAKESPEARE

I wish I'd had Shakespeare's insight decades ago. I now realise that if booze was a moneylender, only the most desperate would do business with the bastard owing to his extortionate interest rates. A few hours' supposed fun in exchange for feeling physically and mentally under par at all other times. Drink, sleep (badly), work (under-performing), repeat, day after day. Interest paid includes the stupid behaviour, broken relationships, wasted money and damage to mental and physical health. I've been trapped in this cycle for decades. The interest is compound, which for many users spirals to the point where the ultimate price is paid.

Suppose a new designer drug comes into circulation. It has identical effects to alcohol. Hospital A and E departments are crowded with the injured and dead due to fights and accidents. Users suffer from organ failure, marriages break down, children are left uncared for, people are dying in their thousands. The situation would cause national panic and the substance would be banned. Yet alcohol is promoted as fun and glamorous. It's used to sell everything from holidays to property developments. You know the kind of thing: photos plastered all over the hoardings of new-build flats, showing a good-looking, happy couple in their new home, glass of wine in hand. Adverts for package holidays showing smiling vacationers holding a glass of vino tinto. And the lead roles in films mostly drink without even getting drunk.

Imagine you're in a social situation. You explain to your friends,

'I've been overdoing the crack cocaine. I'm having a night off.' Are your mates likely to say, 'Oh go on, just a small one'? (I guess that depends on your mates.) Alcohol is one of the most dangerous recreational drugs and yet you have to give an excuse for not using it. Alcohol *is* firewater, and consuming it *is* playing with fire.

Why doesn't the Advertising Standards Authority take a stand against alcohol brands for promoting this highly addictive toxin as fun and glamorous? Maybe they're pissed on the job. Society turns a blind eye to the mayhem caused by drinking because the majority of people are users.

Some people drink because they think it's a rock and roll act of rebellion. As someone with experience of both rebellion and drinking I can confirm it's nothing of the sort. Getting pissed is totally mainstream. And if you are a person who wants to change the world for the better, drinking will only reduce your effectiveness.

In vino veritas. Oh no it isn't. As much bullshit surrounds our culture's relationship with alcohol as comes out of the mouths of those who've drunk it. There are eight bars in Parliament.

I've started to interpret song lyrics in the context of drinking. Bob Marley's 'Redemption Song': 'emancipate yourself from mental slavery. None but ourselves can free our minds'. I guess he's talking of racial politics, but you can take it on many levels. Something that is bad for you and you can't stop doing is called an addiction – that's a form of mental slavery.

I now realise that, paradoxically, swimming makes the drinking possible. It's a semi-antidote to the anxiety, paranoia and depression caused by drinking. It is an unholy alliance which allows me to maintain the habit and to live with a tolerable level of depression.

This realisation moves me closer to giving up swimming altogether so that I can focus full time on the far more important business of drinking. Only joking.

KERBLAM

You may say I'm a dreamer, but I'm not the only one. I hope someday you'll join us. And the world will live as one.

JOHN LENNON

The full moon is striated by horizontal windblown rain. The ferry's mighty engines rumble with the primitive power of hydrocarbon combustion. From the aft upper deck, looking skywards, I see the haze of waste heat, carbon dioxide and water vapour being dumped through twin red funnels into the night air.

High above the sea, out to starboard, I'm hoping to catch a glimpse of the Beasts. I want to familiarise myself with the shoreline, but there's insufficient light for the binoculars and with the naked eye I can only make out shadowy amorphous shapes. As the ship steams into harbour some invisible force sends a shiver down my spine, perhaps the same force which has compelled me to return to these islands. I've come back to the Hebrides, to attempt to swim from the Beasts of Holm to Sandwick Beach on the perimeter of Stornoway.

Next morning I have brain fog, the result of anxiety and trying to sleep in a tent flapping in the Hebridean wind. My first task is to inspect the shoreline along which I plan to swim, and I figure the opposite side of the harbour should provide a good vantage point. So I head for Arnish Point. A little inland of it, set on undulating moorland, I discover an abandoned factory complex in the early stages of decomposition, its wind-blasted steel cladding making ghostly clanking sounds. There are huge rusting steel pipes, girders and the detritus of a place left in a hurry. It has a post-apocalyptic feel. My jangled nerves don't respond well to its macabre feng shui. The place doesn't make sense – why would anyone build huge steel components on an island where raw materials must be imported and the finished product shipped out?

From the factory of doom onwards, the road narrows into a gravel track. I consider getting out of the car and walking, but time is precious. Summer is on its back foot, the days are shortening and the sea temperature dropping. A month of bad weather is possible, and that would scupper the swim.

The Micra and I bounce our way along the rough track. I steer round puddles which might better be described as small lochs. We crest a hill and I see the only buildings on Arnish Point, the peeling white-painted lighthouse and its two keepers' cottages.

Confirming the aphorism 'you only have a job until they invent a machine to do it cheaper', the former residents of these homes lost their jobs in 1971 to an automated buoy out in the harbour. A question crosses my mind: *What are all the loners supposed to do now there are no more jobs for lighthouse keepers?* The cottages are now in private ownership; most likely as second homes, as they are locked and shuttered, yet there are vegetables growing in their walled gardens.

Standing in the lee of the lighthouse, sheltering from the wind and rain, I take an old pair of binoculars from my parka pocket and scan the shoreline on the opposite side of the harbour. There are three bays. One has a rock face behind it where a swimmer would be unable to exit the water. The other two slope back onto shingle beaches and then open moorland; they would provide exit points. The rest of the shoreline consists of steep, dark-coloured rock.

I can't see the Beasts of Holm. Searching for them I scan clockwise, and as I do the place where Kenneth Macphail and the other men drew their last breath comes into view. My heart sinks and anxiety ratchets up a notch as I realise the swim will be longer than I thought.

My binoculars may be old and battered but they are of the highest quality, manufactured by Carl Zeiss. There's a strange and incalculable significance in the fact they are made by the same company which manufactured the periscope through which Commander Lothar von Arnauld, captain of U-boat 35, viewed Kenneth Macphail's ship just before he torpedoed it.

I ask myself why I need to make this swim. At a conscious level I can say it's about a connection with the sea, and that I'm saddened by the injustice of the *Iolaire* disaster. But the real reasons for being here on the limits of the kingdom languish outside the limits of consciousness. It's something primal, and it's taking me way outside my comfort zone. Sleepless nights and rising levels of anxiety make me question my mental state. I do some breathing exercises – which make absolutely no difference. Anxiety buzzes around my head like an angry wasp.

The time has arrived to get close to the scene of the disaster, to feel the energy of the place and see where a swimmer might enter the water. A thirty-minute drive takes me to the opposite side of Stornoway harbour. I park and take a footpath. After a few minutes I crest a hillock and the *Iolaire* monument comes into view. Spindrift carries the smell of the sea inland.

Standing silent guard over its bleak dominion, twenty metres across land and one hundred metres across sea from the Beasts of Holm, the three-metre-high granite structure consists of a plinth carrying formal words of sorrow and remembrance. On that rests an obelisk into the face of which an anchor and crown are chiselled.

My pulse rate has increased. It's as though the energy of that epic battle for survival has embedded itself in the rocks and is in homeopathic solution in the sea. I imagine the wreck underwater, some thirty metres from shore. It's a windy overcast day, intermittently raining, lowish tide. Waves are breaking on the rocks near the monument. Despite being so close to land and only a few miles from Stornoway, the wreck is out of sight of any habitation. Even in daylight this is a bleak place.

I clamber down the rocks towards the water's edge. They slope at thirty degrees, a conglomerate of stones encased in sedimentary rock. The bonding rock is softer and waves have eroded it, leaving the harder stones protruding by up to ten centimetres. Close to the water's edge the rock is covered with slime on which I slip and nearly fall.

These rocks are bone breakers. To be tossed upon their uneven surface by powerful waves would be like throwing dice. An unlucky landing could cause serious injury or death. Throw a six and you are tossed ashore perhaps with only minor injuries. I picture the desperate struggle, but cannot figure out where the men would have attached the line John Macleod swam ashore with.

It was a terrible place to come out of the water that dark night a hundred years ago. And for this swim, even with moderately sized waves and in daylight, it isn't a suitable place to enter the water. Thirty metres east I find a small bay which will provide safe ingress into the sea.

Leaving Holm Point, I walk back across the kilometre or so of undulating sheep-grazed grass towards Stoneyfield Farm, following in the footsteps of the survivors who found shelter there. I pick my way through a thicket of prickly gorse bushes, which would not have been so easy to dodge that dark night a century ago. I picture the injured, arm in arm, limping, bloody and shivering. As soon as they started stumbling into the farm, its owners had the good sense to open their curtains so other survivors could see their lights and find their way to shelter. I ignore the barking dogs and knock on the door. No one is in.

In this small island community I have to ask only a couple of people before I get a contact for Colin Macleod (no relation of John Macleod). A broad-shouldered man, he looks as though he's built for sea swimming, for which he has celebrity status on Lewis after an impressive but ultimately failed attempt to swim the Minch. Through no fault of his own, after swimming some 30 miles, his support boat lost contact with him and therefore made a distress call which precipitated a search and rescue operation. His crossing of the Minch went from a challenge to a battle for survival.

Colin was unfazed, and as night fell he calmly continued swimming for a lighthouse on the mainland. He believes he would have reached it, but his conviction was never tested because, thanks to the little red light on his tow-float, he was eventually spotted by the coastguard helicopter. The chopper recruited a rescue boat from the *Loch Seaforth*, the same ferry I arrived on, which pulled Colin from the sea. The rescue made front page news in the *Stornoway Gazette*, which I could tell was a source of embarrassment to him.

Colin puts the mess-up in the Minch down to poor planning (not his planning), and though he seems keen to accompany me on the swim, I realise I'll have to convince him it's been planned properly. One thing we won't have to worry about is losing contact with our support boat – we don't have one. This is why we'll be wearing wetsuits, which will increase our survival time in the cold water, and a tow-float which will make us visible and will provide buoyancy in an emergency.

I haven't worn the wetsuit for over a year, so testing the thing seems a sensible idea. The next day is stormy so I find a sheltered bay for a practice swim. I pull the neoprene over my legs and arms but can't get the back zip done up. I quickly realise this is because my stomach has grown. No matter how hard I pull, contort myself and throw myself about while sucking my gut in, the zip won't cooperate. A funny sight for anyone watching, but I feel humiliated.

After a comedy ten minutes I get the thing closed. I look down at my rubber-covered belly, the bastard, and I feel a sense of self-loathing – the saboteur is clearly back in business.

My emotions are all over the place. I have a will to get in the water but it's competing with fear. Finally I pluck up the courage and am about to plunge myself in when a dog walker comes into sight. In the nicest possible way he expresses his concern that it's not safe to swim in this storm.

He's a friendly, likeable guy in his early thirties with a hipster beard. We chat. His name is Peter. He's ex-army and now works as winch-man on the coastguard helicopter. I assure him my swim will be safe and I will stay close to shore. He accepts this, but when I tell him about the Beasts to Sandwich Bay swim he looks concerned.

***

The next morning Colin and I reach the *Iolaire* monument before dawn. It's chilly and dark, but the eastern sky is glowing with the promise of a new day. The weather forecast is fair and we're in luck, the sea is almost flat. The tide is rising and I feel a deep sense of optimism. Not just about the swim but about life in general.

Colin and I sit in silence on boulders on the shingle beach waiting for night to become day. We're lost in our own thoughts. From the profile of the shoreline I figure the only place the current could be problematic is over the Beasts themselves. There's one way to find out for sure.

By seven o'clock there's sufficient light. Colin is first in. The sea temperature is 10 °C. In the wetsuit, cold is limited to the bits of body not covered in rubber: hands, feet and face. I was expecting the feelings of doom to return, but they don't come. Perhaps that's because I'm with Colin. He is a matter-of-fact, no-nonsense guy who instils confidence. None the less I have given Isabelle, a friend in London, details of the swim. If I don't phone her by 8.30 she'll call the coastguard.

To help prevent calamities a marker has been built on top of the Beasts, and though the skerry itself is now covered by the rising tide the marker protrudes from the sea surface. As we swim slowly out of the bay it comes into sight and we track towards it. Out in the middle of the harbour, about a mile away, we see the *Loch Seaforth* leaving Lewis bound for Ullapool. For any of its passengers who happened to be looking across the harbour in our direction, we would be tiny specks in the distance and they would almost certainly not see us.

We swim directly over the wreck of the *Iolaire*. Many of the bodies of those who died were never recovered and some may remain inside her rusting hull. I peer down into the depths but the water isn't clear and I can't see the wreck, for which I'm thankful. I'd rather her seaweed-covered hull remained a mystery.

As we approach the Beasts I see dark rock rising up from the murky depths. I think of the screaming sound survivors reported as the vessel's iron hull rode up this unyielding surface. Colin and I pause for a while, floating above their menacing form. I feel no angry ghosts, and Colin seems relaxed so I'm thinking he doesn't either. Though I like and trust him, we haven't had time to get to know each other, and so I'm reluctant to let him into my inner thoughts.

On Lewis, even though a century has passed since the *Iolaire* disaster, there often follows an awkward silence whenever it's mentioned. I'd planned to pen some words and leave them floating on a piece of paper above the wreck. But there are no words on paper, because in the previous days I found I'd also gone mute, writing was impossible.

We leave the Beasts heading north and I'm relieved to feel the soothing rhythm of swimming. Fortune has smiled upon us. It is rarely this calm in the Hebrides. Every ten minutes or so we stop briefly to check our position and Colin takes photos with his waterproof camera. Cormorants with their rapid wing cadence pass close over our heads. Young herring gulls hover, checking out these misplaced rubber-clad mammals.

We are two hundred metres out, parallel with the craggy eastern shoreline. When I swing my head left I see the distant western shoreline and Arnish Point lighthouse. The wetsuit may protect me from the cold but it feels unnatural; I'm too buoyant and can't get traction in the water.

As we draw level with Stoneyfield Farm, the rising sun bursts out through a gap between hill and cloud, putting the farm into silhouette. It's as though events are being choreographed, that there is a higher authority at work, that we are not alone.

Kerblam. As we continue north I am hit by a sudden wall of exhaustion. This shouldn't be a physically taxing swim, but a voice says, *I can't go on*. In the previous month I've been drinking again but I've been sober for a week, since when I've been feeling under the weather. This could be alcohol withdrawal or perhaps a virus. The 'can't go on' voice is answered by another which says, *you must carry on, you have no choice.*

This has suddenly become a battle of wills. Where my stomach should be there's a void, the fuel tank is empty, I'm running on fumes. Every movement requires willpower. But there's no way I'm giving up. A thought crosses my mind, *this would be a beautiful place to die.* It would however be inconvenient for Colin, who'd have to deal with my corpse.

I keep going, only slower. My connection with land feels fractured; time is also fragmenting. There is only sea. I consider telling Colin how I feel, but I wouldn't know how to express it.

Colin stops and is pointing. I see nothing, turn through 360 degrees and look back in the direction of his outstretched finger. She surfaces. A beautiful woman with piercing emerald-green eyes, her golden curls protruding from a grey swim cap. She is five metres away, smiling at me. Her broad shoulders and well-defined collar bones are clear of the water. 'What a gorgeous smile. She's definitely flirting with me.'

I stare at her, wide eyed, through untinted goggles. She reminds me of Harry, my 'nun' friend. My mind struggles to process the information. Someone swimming out here on the margins of the kingdom, at this time of day, at this time of year seems unlikely. I hit reset and put my face back in the sea. When I look up she's gone. In her place there's a seal. I look at Colin, trying to gauge his reaction. He's smiling the smile of a man who's just seen a seal. I don't let on what I saw.

Such creatures may not be common, but I was never in any doubt of their existence in these outlying islands. In her seal skin the selkie has a small grey head with large eyes and whiskers set on in a rubbery cute doglike face.

The exhaustion evaporates. I'm back to normal, if anything about this can be considered normal. She watches us closely, sometimes raising her head high out of the water. Some people believe the souls of dead people inhabit animals. A mystic submariner, she is the opposite of a predatory submarine captain. She's not here to sink us, but to keep us safe.

I can't remember ever having felt calmer. Time is no longer fragmenting, it no longer exists. We swim on. I'm in a state of bliss. Everything about being in this place at this time is right. Everything is beautiful. Fear is banished. The saboteur is neutralised. Ego has disappeared. Arms move, legs kick, body rolls, there is breathing. As we continue north, the dark rocky shoreline moves slowly at exactly the same speed in the opposite direction. I have a picture of us viewed from high above, three souls unseen by any other life form. We are in a vast universe, moving slowly, almost imperceptibly, through this clean Caledonian water.

Stoneyfield Farm is now behind us and on shore there are a few houses, which means we're approaching Stornoway. Keeping direction has been difficult because our destination has been too far away to see, so no doubt we've zigzagged our way north. Surfacing and diving, scarcely making a ripple, effortlessly moving through her domain, the selkie keeps watch over us.

The penny drops. I wanted to make a connection with wise ancestors. I was curious how it would feel to be in their proximity. I imagined I might feel anger for the injustice they endured, not only their death by sinking but also for their forced exposure to the killing fields of war. But anger hasn't visited, and I'm certain this has something to do with the selkie. She's an emissary, although it's not so much a message she carries, but rather a feeling, a way of being.

Sunrise over Stoneyfield Farm, photo Colin Macleod.

The *Iolaire*'s passengers had witnessed a bellyful of broken minds and bodies. And, after their untimely death by sinking, they've borne silent witness from up on high to plenty more barbarism in our world. Now, in our time, they witness strange and dangerous waves of polarising psychic energy. But these are not angry ancestors. They are calm and wise, and I'm hungry for their wisdom.

How, I could not say – perhaps through psychic osmosis – but on this return visit to Lewis I was hoping I might absorb their knowledge, which I imagined would take the form of reasoned learning. But what's actually happening is simpler and easier to grasp. It's a blissful way of being in which violence and unkindness, let alone war, would be impossible. In this state of mind I couldn't be roused to hostility, or to its close associate, hatred. Nor would I be likely to produce such a response in anyone else.

The scale of the surroundings bring about a sense of perspective. I see myself as tiny and insignificant and it feels liberating. I am a drop in the ocean. The pressure to be something or somebody has evaporated.

We continue north. Sandwick Bay is getting closer. It seems appropriate that we should pass the large cemetery which slops down to its southern quadrant, where bodies washed up after the *Iolaire* disaster, and where a number of the dead are buried.

Colin is a faster swimmer than I. As we approach the beach he is ahead. He stops and insists I get out of the water first. I think he feels this is the gentlemanly thing to do, and though I'm not concerned who is first out, I feel it is gentlemanly to accept his kindness.

My feet meet seabed and I walk unsteadily from the sea onto the dark shingle beach. Gravity is stronger than I remembered. The transition from floating to standing is too sudden and feels disorientating. Colin and I look at each other, smile and high five. We look back out into the bay. The selkie is gone.

***

Struggling to return my mind to worldly affairs, I remember I should phone Isabelle in London. I look at my watch. I have absolutely no idea what it will say. We could have been in the water an hour or many hours. The watch says 08.20. The swim has taken longer than expected. If Isabelle were to call the coastguard it would be highly embarrassing, especially for Colin. My hands are cold and I fumble to open my tow-float and recover the phone. By the time I do it's 08.25. Cold wet fingers won't operate the screen. 08.27. I dry my hands. 08.28. I dial the wrong number. 08.29. I try again and this time get through. Isabelle is distressed. 'Are you OK?' she says. I explain I have no idea why the swim took us longer than expected. My mind feels like cotton wool. I can't think clearly. I promise to call her back.

Colin appears to have taken our adventure in his stride. After all, this swim is small fry compared to the Minch, a swim which he achieves the following summer, only the second person ever to have done so. I thank him for coming, he thanks me for inviting him, we give each other an awkward man-hug. He drives off to work in his big red Transit van. I call a taxi and return to my little green car. Our goodbye seems inadequate, but such is the unsatisfactory nature of human relations. I feel as calm as a flat windless sea.

My account may make you question my mental state or wonder if I had taken drugs. There were no drugs. As for my mental state, I've seldom felt better, but many a madman must have said the same.

MUM

In Stornoway Town my temporary sleeping place is a tent in the garden of the Heb Hostel. The place is run by Christine and her dad Tosh, whose friendliness permeates the whole establishment and creates a cosy social environment, where, in my newfound state of mental calm, I find I'm popular amongst the other guests. Though I know both the calm and the sobriety are temporary, after the swim I feel more at peace than ever before – and I haven't felt the urge to drink since arriving on the island.

My sister calls and tells me our mum isn't well, I should get myself to Yorkshire asap. The next morning I drive aboard the *Loch Seaforth*, cross the Minch, and drive south.

Three days later I look out of Mum's bedroom window and see a large bird of prey circling nearby. It's a red kite. My sister, my niece-in-law and I are with Mum as she takes her final breaths. She takes her last one at ten past three that afternoon, aged ninety-three.

I'm not able to find words to express how I feel about Mum's death, which makes me think of the silence surrounding the *Iolaire* disaster. The right words are hard to find. Maybe they don't exist.

POSTSCRIPT-SKELETON

I started acting like a cunt in 1975. I forgot to stop. I do feel ashamed.

Lines delivered by the character Elton John from the film *Rocketman*

After Mum's death the writing ran itself onto the rocks. Taking on water at an alarming rate, it looked like the book might sink altogether. But now, two years later, the time has come to pump the bilges and re-float this manuscript.

A lot has happened. There have been pink clouds and dead seals; I've accidentally become a human torpedo, and failed to attempt to save someone's life, to mention just a few, and I haven't swum for many months.

It was new year's morning. I'd gone to bed rat-arsed. The screams outside at 4 a.m. did wake me, but I immediately fell asleep again. Next morning I found a trail of blood in the corridor outside my flat. I followed it to my neighbour's front door, from whom I learned her friend had been viciously stabbed and had nearly died from a punctured lung. I felt disgusted with myself for not being there to give first aid.

That was the last time I drank – two years and two months ago. It's been a rollercoaster of highs and lows, but this time round I wasn't sailing uncharted waters. Those individual months without alcohol had equipped me with the basic navigation skills needed to cross the stormy sea of temptation into the only slightly less windblown ocean of abstinence.

***

A few months into giving up alcohol a friend who was also in the early stages of sobriety described herself as being on the Pink Cloud. I'd never heard of it. Looking it up I realised it matched my experience. Pink Cloud Syndrome describes a sense of euphoria which can occur in the early months or years of drug cessation. I experienced a textbook case of it. It's dangerous because it offers a false sense of security. If I'd done my homework I'd have been pre-warned a fall was on the way, that inevitably I was going to crash out of the crimson ball of water vapour, hit the ground and have to face the shit I'd been running from during my decades of alcohol abuse.

The fall from the Pink Cloud nearly tipped me off the wagon. Had I been to Alcoholics Anonymous I would no doubt have been forewarned, but my mistrust of institutions had kept me away despite a number of friends' insistence I should go.

Out jogging, I turned a corner and nearly ran headlong into an alpha male travelling in the opposite direction. His perfectly trimmed beard and designer tracksuit spoke of preening and mirrors. There were definitely no spiders up this guy's nose, yet the uncertainty on his face suggested an image self-policed with such care he dared not smile for fear the mask might slip. This encounter made me think of my own mask and realise I'm not hiding behind one anymore. Alcohol was the elastic holding it in place. Without it I feel like a man who's just shaved his big bushy beard. It's a relief. Hiding took energy.

If authenticity is being honest about your feelings and who you are, I realise there are still many authentic people left in this crazy world. They are called children. Henry David Thoreau said, 'The tragedy of a person's life is what dies inside them while they're alive.' He's right: school and the System eventually take their toll. I also have to take responsibility for becoming the assassin of my own soul, and drinking was part of that murderous mission. But I'd been lucky, because rather than dying it looks like it had gone into a persistent vegetative state – from which it now emerges, somewhat uncertain, shaking and bleary eyed, like a bear waking after a winter of hibernation.

***

But this born-again bumbling bear was unknowingly being stalked by an acronym. PAWS: Post Acute Withdrawal Syndrome. It can last for two years; that's how long it can take for a heavy user's brain chemistry to recover. Symptoms include depression, anxiety, confusion, and difficulty in multi-tasking. I experienced all of them, especially depression worse than ever before. It was horrible and it still re-emerges. Had I been to AA I would have learned about PAWS too, but the foreknowledge of a two-year struggle would most likely have acted as a disincentive. So I choose to see my naivety as an enabling factor. A case of the lack of knowledge being power.

After a year and a half sober I realised I'm not the person I thought I was, not the person the drinking me had been trying to be. I'm quieter than I thought I was. Turns out that I never really wanted to be that James Bond character with the Martini lifestyle after all.

This might sound like an identity crisis, but it's not. What I was living with before I sobered up was such. I was living a life that didn't belong to me. No wonder I was confused. I wonder, how many other people are living placebo lives? The transition from the former me to the new me seems to have been relatively smooth, but identity is something we industrial humans struggle with. I count myself lucky it hasn't yet developed into a full-blown crisis.

***

At about a year sober I spotted a drowning teenager. There were no heroics; all I had to do was tell a lifeguard who paddled out on his board and rescued him. Had it been the drinking me on the beach that day, with my compromised powers of perception, I don't believe I'd have noticed, and the kid would have slipped underwater unseen. That's two skins saved by stopping drinking: the kid's and my own.

Then there was the pandemic. Pretty soon I got ill. I lost my taste and smell for a short time. I recovered, but the next time I swam was unlike any other. It was a horrible experience. My body told me to remove myself from the water and I was listening. It was a very short swim. I tried again the following day. This time I barely got in up to my waist and walked straight out without swimming at all. Something is different. It feels as though my physiology has changed. My body now says a definitive no to cold. It was summer before I swam again and even at 16 °C the water was too cold. I swam for forty-five minutes, from which it took me a week to recover. These days I swim infrequently and only for 10 minutes or so.

So what, you may ask, am I now doing in Kent, walking into the winter sunrise across a mile of flat sand at Greatstone Beach? As I step into the sea I look up at twelve square metres of brightly coloured fabric hovering above my head. I feel something wriggle from under my bare foot. A small fish jumps clear of the surface and is gone, an escape strategy programmed by millions of years of evolution. For humans, skimming across the sea on a surfboard pulled by a kite is not evolved behaviour, and that is perhaps why it frightens the hell out of me. Yet though I'm shitting bricks I know this activity has the potential to be life changing, and wearing a thick wetsuit means I don't feel cold at all.

My first attempt at kitesurfing was nearly my last. I lost control of the kite which sped low across the sky creating a huge amount of power, pulling me off my feet. Up I went and then down, towed through the water at a depth of perhaps a foot like a von Arnauld torpedo. Instead of letting go of the control bar I pulled on it, producing even more power. Eventually I surfaced, choking and terrified. My confidence was seriously knocked and I considered giving up. But like the swimming I've been persistent. Obsessive even.

Months of stormy winter weather followed by lockdown put the kibosh on this new addiction. But post-lockdown I'm back at Greatstone. About to enter the water after walking across a mile of sand, I notice something greyish ahead of me. It's a baby seal. She galumphs a few metres, then exhausted she stops, rests, and repeats. She must have been stranded at high tide. It would have taken her hours chasing the retreating waterline. But she's nearly there, and after another few minutes her Herculean effort is rewarded. She disappears into the surf, leaving me wondering if she'll find her mum.

A couple of weeks later and I'm back on the same beach. This time, on my way out of the sea, I notice a skeleton on the high water line. I look closer. It's a baby seal. I'm the only person to have witnessed this drama. It's a reminder of the fragility of life. I almost cry, but still being an emotionally blocked male tears don't come.

One morning twenty years ago I woke with a pain in my knee. Over the following days other joints became affected until my whole body was wracked with a pain that proved to be arthritis. It was as if I'd suddenly been given an indeterminate sentence of torture. I did consider suicide. I was lucky. Over the following two years the arthritis gradually burned itself out. But a memory that sticks with me from that time is lying on the living room floor watching the TV, transfixed by images of people skimming across a turquoise sea towed by brightly coloured kites. At that time I could barely walk let alone kitesurf, but the seed of interest in kitesurfing remained.

From idea to actuality in two decades – an impressive level of procrastination. But, like the one-month periods of abstinence paved the way for long-term sobriety, so the swimming has prepared me for kitesurfing. I feel comfortable in the water, leaving one less thing to be frightened of.

***

I may no longer be quaffing from the chalice of poison but my other nemesis, ADHD, is still alive and kicking.

involuntary and frustrating tuning-out or absence of mind; difficulty concentrating; being bored easily, beginning one thing but going on to another before completing the first; problems keeping order physically in one's room, on one's desk, in one's car; difficulty being on time, poor impulse control, manifested in speaking out of turn, interrupting others in conversation . . .

This could so easily describe the life of an alcoholic, and it certainly describes mine, but these are actually some of the symptoms of attention deficit hyperactivity disorder as reported by Gabor Maté in *Scattered Minds*. Reading his book I realise the effect of long-term drinking closely mimics that of ADHD.

Albert Einstein said that 'time is what prevents everything happening at once'. Not so for people with ADHD, for whom everything does indeed happen at once. Like a songbird chasing insects, thoughts and emotions dart about so rapidly they might as well all be happening simultaneously. I often find clumps of seaweed tangled with fishing line on the beach. This is a physical representation of my mind.

Two years sober, I can see that using alcohol was like pouring petrol on the fire of my existing problems. A person with compromised impulse control who then takes a drug which increases impulsivity is heading for trouble. Elton John's character in *Rocketman* reports that he began 'acting like a cunt in 1975' and forgot to stop being one. Something he feels ashamed of. Ditto for me, and with a similar timeline.

Sitting on a train at a standstill next to another stationary train, when one train moves off it's at first impossible to know which train is moving. Like such a passenger, as a drinker with ADHD I felt a similar sense of psychic disorientation – was it me or the rest of the world that was moving? Or both?

An impaired sense of time means that carrying out tasks requiring a sequence of many steps create a feeling of panic. Without booze my perception still feels jumbled, but less so, and where I was ignoring multi-step tasks now I am now tackling them. I'm also beginning to develop an understanding of my limitations and learning to forgive myself for them.

During more than two years of abstinence there have been positive changes in my psyche and physique. Through this I've come to see how a person's entire morphology is changed by years of heavy drinking. Body mass, colour and texture of skin, eyes and voice, everything physical is impacted. The psychological ramifications, though less visible, are no less profound.

As the most significant activities in my life, first there was drinking, then there was swimming and drinking, then there was swimming and not drinking. Now there's kitesurfing and not drinking. Time may be what prevents everything happening at once, but while kitesurfing there is so much happening at once that a compromised sense of time doesn't matter. Perhaps it's even an advantage. The activity harnesses a need for exhilaration and adventure and provides focus for an over-active mind. Most importantly, after kitesurfing I feel a profound sense of peace as I did after the Beasts of Holm swim.

James Baldwin wrote, 'not everything that is faced can be changed, but nothing can be changed until it is faced'. I count myself lucky, not only because I somehow found the strength to face alcohol, but also because by facing it change is underway. This doesn't mean alcohol no longer poses a threat, but I can now see that alcohol was never *the problem*, rather addiction is actually a symptom of my issues from childhood. A sensible person would have read a book to find this out. I've had to write one.

Boatyards are full of unfulfilled dreams, project boats which never get finished. Projects which are eventually ended when the yard finally breaks up the rotting dream and unceremoniously dumps it in a skip. The writing of this book could so easily have turned into similarly truncated dream. No one could be more surprised than me that these words have gone from dream to reality.

Gradually is a concept which cropped up early on in this book. When I started writing it my life was gradually falling apart, and hope was in short supply. Today, as I pen these final words, the tide has turned. Life is gradually getting better, and hope is returning.

THE END

Printed in Great Britain
by Amazon

40357826R00121